IT DON'T MEAN A THING, IF IT AIN'T GOT THAT SWING!

This book is dedicated to Lucie Makowiecka and William Jameson Snow.

First published in Great Britain 1976 by Dempsey & Squires (Publishers) Ltd., 8 Berwick Street, London W.1.

GLENN MILLER

& the Age of Swing

Conceived, designed and produced by : *GEORGE SNOW*
Written by : *JONATHON GREEN*
Photo Research : *BRUCE SAWFORD & GEORGE SNOW*
Personal Assistant to Mr. Snow : *NICK MARSHALL*
Personal Assistant to Mr. Snows Assistant: *MILLARD ZIADE*

Typeset in 11/13pt Plantin Roman by: *TOTTENHAM TYPESETTERS*
Captions set in 8/8pt Univers by : *GEOFFREY MARSH*
ISBN No. : *0-86044-007-9*

CONTENTS

'In God We Trust' said the monster dollars of Busby Berkeley's 'Gold-diggers of 1933'. In due course FDR would back up the Lord with the New Deal. In the meantime, escape artists like Berkeley helped keep the national mind off the Depression.

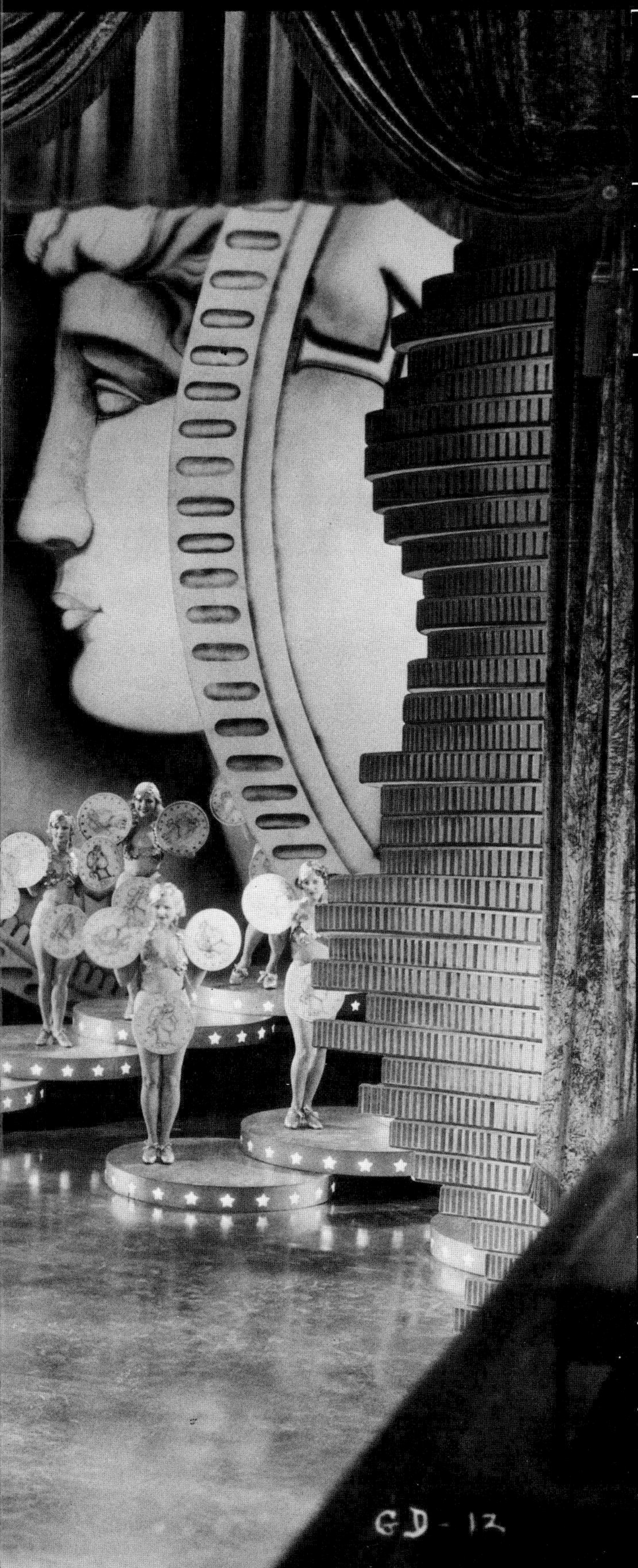

CHAPTER ONE

TIME OF THEIR LIVES

IT WAS AN AGE of desperation. From 1929's Crash and the Depression that followed to 1939's Declaration of War in Europe. French poet and diplomat Paul Claudel summed it up aptly in a Washington visit, midsummer 1931. 'Gentlemen,' he declared, 'in the little moment that remains to us between the crisis and the catastrophe, we may as well drink a glass of champagne.'

The economists and political pundits may have made their grim prophecies long before Wall Street collapsed in October 1929 and gave the showbiz weekly *Variety* an immortal headline—'Wall Street Lays an Egg'—but no-one was listening. The War to End Wars had been fought. Millions had been sacrificed to make a better world, one that would be safe for democracy, a land fit for heroes . . . all the pious platitudes of an exhausted post-war generation of survivors. Bright Young People both sides of the Atlantic led the race towards all-out fun and games. Skirts rushed up from the ankles towards the thighs, the long hair of domestic servitude gave way to the Eton bobs of liberation. The waltz was replaced by the Charleston or the Black Bottom, both names redolent of the faintly naughty ambience of the Twenties, a world which was condemned by its elders as frankly perverse. Their strictures made no difference to a younger generation who had watched elder brothers march off to die and were determined to make sure that they, at least, had their fun before it was time for them to go.

When the economy collapsed one Friday in October 1929 and formerly well-heeled stock speculators queued to jump from their thirtieth floor windows, the good times were over. Maybe they had only been the thinnest of illusory good times, but for a while, in the ghastly aftermath of the Great War, they had turned people's minds from their miseries. But with the Crash came horrors of new and even more miserable situation. And unlike the War, no-one could claim exemption. Millionaires found themselves peddling apples on the very streets where they had once wheeled and dealed their fortunes. Small farmers from the Mid-West suddenly faced the terrors of migration. They left their old homes and trekked hopelessly towards California to pick up the minimal wages available for fruit-picking. The Okies, ex-Oklahoma farmers whose plight was epitomised in John Steinbeck's 'Grapes of Wrath', became the symbol of the migrant workers who scratched for their living. One moved, worked for enough money to move on, worked again in the new place, moved on; it was unremitting. Across America, and thence to Europe, already dependent on the New World, poverty spread like a creeping forest fire. Governments rose and fell on their abilities to deal with the Depression. Desperate people looked to new leaders to take them out of their troubles. New Messiahs arose: the glorious myths of Stalin's Communist Russia, the apparent successes of Fascism in Germany and Italy. If the old order had brought this misery, then, so many people hoped, novelty acts might prove the political winners.

Desperation meant many things to the millions who suffered under the post-Depression problems. Some queued day after day at the employment agencies where perhaps 5,000

ABOVE: **President in the making, Dwight D. Eisenhower led tanks, guns and troops in a rehearsal for his European campaign.** *FACING PAGE:* **Franklin D. Roosevelt – proponent of the Great American Dream's second chance, better known as 'The New Deal'.**

applications per day might try to grab at the slim 300 jobs available. It was, inevitably, a formative era for trades union organising. In England, where the 1926 General Strike was still a vivid memory in every mind, thousands marched from Jarrow in the North-East, poorest of the poor areas, to demand work in

ABOVE: **General Douglas MacArthur, future hero of the Pacific, quashed irate veterans at the Battle of the Anacostia Flats. Hoover watched from the White House as the Welfare Army got theirs.**

London. In America the labour movement mobilised and set out under its unconquerable leader John L. Lewis to get the equal rights that an entrenched capitalist system refused to offer. Veterans of the First World War, the Bonus Army as they were known, marched to make their demonstration in Washington. In the Battle of Anacostia Flats on July 28th, 1932, the veterans were literally smashed to pieces by a force of regular troops and national guard under the command of General MacArthur, the future hero of the Pacific, and a Major Dwight D. Eisenhower as his second in command. It was, no doubt, ideal training for the man who led America through the paranoid fifties. At the head of cavalry, infantry, machine guns, tanks and guns, MacArthur and Eisenhower directed the brutal attack on the 8,600 veterans encamped within view of the hapless President Hoover struggling for re-election from an unpopular White House. As the cripples, the women and the children fled their pitiful 'Hooverville' of cardboard shacks, some already burning from the fires set by the troops, Hoover declared 'A challenge to the authority of the U.S. Government has been met.' It must have given the battered vets some comfort when the electorate tossed Hoover out a few months later.

Paradoxically the Washington police, under Chief Pelham D. Glassford, had been relatively sympathetic to the veterans. Police across the country had less tolerance for the massive worker demonstrations, strikes and sit-ins—which represented the hardcore struggle against the bosses and the poverty they had helped create, and were now refusing to alleviate. Pointyhead liberals in New York and Hollywood's writing community might support labour, and indeed Communism, but for the mass of the people looking on, the struggles of organised labour were just a step away from the Red Terror. Hysterical radio demagogues like Father Charles Coughlin railed against Russia, international Jewry, and organised labour; Roosevelt, he announced, was a mixture of George III and Simon Legree, the slaveholding bad guy of 'Uncle Tom's Cabin.' So America watched as union pickets and company goons fought out their struggles across the land. The bosses remained secure, safe within their status, as they forced worker to fight worker in the time honoured manner. Miners, steel workers, automobile makers, barbers, hosiers, and seamen, workers from every stratum of the job market realised that striking, with or without violence, was the only way to get what they wanted. The big strikes, miners, steel and cars, were the most savage, but their sacrifices and struggles made the way easier for the lesser unions to make their point. By the end of the Thirties organised labour was more than just an American branch of Communism, to be feared and fought. Faced with the desperate years, the unions had given a little more flesh to the cherished myth that in the Land of Opportunity everyone was entitled to his share of the national prosperity. Far from being tentacles of anarchy, the American unions created a position that was, and remains, essentially conservative. What mattered, however, was that everyone did indeed get their slice of the cake. Formerly those who had it weren't interested, once successful, in handing anything out. The labour struggles of the Thirties didn't really deprive the bosses, but they just let the hungry workers in on the act.

On March 4, 1933, Franklin Delano Roosevelt was confirmed as America's 32nd President. That very morning the continuing economic collapse closed the doors of every bank in the nation. The country was terrified as never before. FDR, as the new president, was soon to become known, set himself the task of allaying those fears and replacing them with a new optimism. In his first hundred days in office he formulated the 'New Deal,' a series of major reforms that changed American life as radically as the most revolutionary voices might demand, and, in time, rather more so than they actually wanted. For the first time since October 1929's terrible Black Friday when 16 million shares tumbled into chaos, the American people felt they had a man in charge who was going to get them out of this mess. He may have been dictatorial in his style, but his famous radio broadcasts, the 'Fireside Chats', had the same morale boosting effects as those of Winston Churchill, another popular dictator, were to have less than a decade later and three thousand miles away.

Central to the new deal was FDR's appreciation that if the crippled capitalist system couldn't provide all the jobs required, then a strong government would have to provide its own remedies. With this government intervention in mind, FDR created what become known as the Alphabet Agencies, government work-creation programmes. The NRA, CCC, PWA and WPA took over the plight of the American unemployed and between them attempted to solve the problems FDR and his nation were facing. The NRA (National Recovery Administration) came top of the list. Designed to regulate wages, prices and working hours it was advertised by its Blue Eagle symbol and attracted huge support. The CCC, (Civilian Conservation Corps), was essentially an agency of public works. Even the fiercest opponents of the NRA—businessmen who called it creeping socialism and socialists who called it business fascism—had to acknowledge the uses of this backed programme of good works. Some 2.5 million young unemployed men were taken off the

Fashion Park

Double-breasted "Park Lounge" ..first fashion choice for Spring. Notice wide shoulders, full drape chest, fitted waist ... distinction! ... In the choicest new worsteds.

"Stanerect"... an Original, an Exclusive! Makes short men look tall, stout men look slender. In fabrics of noteworthy character.

"Park Lounge". New ease. New freedom. New assurance. The 1937 idea, finely hand-tailored, in fabrics of uncommon smartness. Leadership!

SUITS $45 to $100
TOPCOATS $40 to $125
FASHION PARK, ROCHESTER, N. Y

streets and out of the employment queues. They were paid $30 a month, often sent automatically to their parents at home, and set to work on a massive list of ecological activities. The conservation and reafforestation undeniably gave an enormous boost to the overall health of America's physical resources.

The Public Works Administration (PWA) was another way of using the unemployed for the benefit of the nation. An army of working men was recruited for public works projects of every type and in every state. They built bridges, railroad tracks, water tanks, government offices, prisons, dams and so on. During the New Deal era some 35% of the new hospitals, 65% of the city halls and 70% of the schools and colleges were the work of the PWA. To boost the PWA, FDR created the WPA (the Works Progress Administration) which did more than merely finance the public building, the role of the PWA. The WPA took over the day to day administration of the programme. It added another side to its workings: large-scale patronage of the arts. Paying wages of up to $94.90 a month, the WPA gathered into its ranks a whole mass of artists, actors, musicians and writers all of whom used their talents for the public good. John Steinbeck himself worked for the WPA for a while, taking a census of dogs in Monterey, California. In 1939 he summed up the Depression for all time in 'The Grapes of Wrath'.

But the New Deal on the one hand and the labour struggles on the other weren't enough to alleviate the miseries of the Depression for everyone. After all, when all was said and done, neither way of improving life actually gave anyone any more than the solid average standard of living that had been taken as a matter of course before the Crash. For some enterprising people this simply wasn't enough. There were ways of making money, plenty of money, that didn't put you on a picket line or into a job with the Alphabet Agencies. Crime, always a good payer, proliferated across the country.

There were two varieties of criminal in the American thirties. And one or two specialists. Essentially the gangsters split between the organised mobs of the cities (hangovers from the great burgeoning of the mobs in the rich days of Prohibition), and the loners of the sticks. Arthur—Dutch Schultz—Fleigenheimer, Legs Diamond (ex-boss of the Hotsy-Totsy Club in New York), Salvatore Lucania (who preferred the name 'Lucky' Luciano), Bugsy Seigel and others were the hard core city mobsters. With millions of dollars 'profit' between them they became the first generation of American gangsters to realise that with a little grease applied to the right governmental and authoritarian palms, there was no reason why their operations should not go on with a minimum of friction. Why fight, either against the government or each other, when they could do so much better for themselves as just one more aspect, perhaps slightly more obviously grubby than its more legitimate branches, of American capitalism.

ABOVE: **Bonnie and Clyde, uglier than the movie. "We rob banks!"**

The loners of the Mid- and South-West were another style of criminal altogether. In the style of their predecessors, the gangsters of the 'Wild West', these picturesque loners carved out their bloody and short-lived careers through their poverty stricken states. None of them ever became exceptionally rich, their crimes, while always well publicised and often oozing blood, were never much above stickups and small-town bank robberies. Ma Barker and her boys, Clyde Barrow and Bonnie Parker, George 'Machine Gun' Kelly, Lester Gillis and Baby Face Nelson, John Dillinger . . . these were the names who symbolised small-time rural crime in the Thirties. Charles A. 'Pretty Boy' Floyd is as good an example as any. At the age of 18 Floyd started his criminal career with a Post Office heist that netted him $350 in pennies. For the next dozen years he pillaged some 30 Midwestern banks. He carved ten notches on his pocket watch for the men he had killed. Like the rest of his Midwest desperado contemporaries, Floyd got his deserts in the end when the FBI caught up

ABOVE: Charles Lindbergh. American heroics in person.

with him. In October 1934 he was tracked down to an Ohio Farm where the G-men (Government men as the Federal Bureau of Investigation agents were popularly known) gunned him down.

The FBI, under its holier-than-thou, cleaner than clean boss J. Edgar Hoover, set out to purge the Thirties gangsters. They compiled the still publicised Public Enemies List; John Dillinger was the first to hit the top of the charts. Hoover, as Director, realised that his new agency (it was formed in 1924 and had reached its crime-busting heights by the new decade), had to maintain an image in *fact* as well as popular fiction of utterly scrupulous rectitude. If the Thirties had any heroes then the G-men surely filled the role. As daring as the gangsters and hoods they fought, with the added bonus of being 'the good guys', Hoover and trusted lieutenants such as Elliott Ness of the celebrated 'Untouchables', so called for their immunity both from death and corruption, stood up in American eyes as the ideal figures to worship.

Crime bulked large, whether from the criminal or the cop point of view, in the Thirties. And when evil touched the nation's number one hero, then the country was able to revel, righteously appalled, in what had to be the crime of the decade: the Lindbergh kidnapping. For all his leanings towards fascism and generally accelerated eccentricity, Charles Lindbergh, pioneer transatlantic flier, was an almost unrivalled top dog in America's pantheon of contemporary heroes. When, on March 1, 1932, the flier received a kidnapping demand for his baby son, the whole nation reeled with him from the shock. It was not for another four years that the kidnapper met his death in the electric chair. But before that Bruno Hauptman, the barely literate kidnapper, had killed the baby six weeks after taking it, and had spent his way through most of the $50,000 ransom money put up by Lindy. As Hauptman fried in the chair, the whole nation breathed a sigh of relief and undisguised delight.

In an era of desperation and depression people inevitably had to have some way out of the miseries. Getting a job, working for the government, or turning to crime helped many cope with unpleasant realities, but there was a much simpler way out. Industry may have been suffering in the Thirties, but there was one area of business in which things had never been so good. The media, prime provider of escape from the problems of real life, boomed in this Depression era as never before. Whether it was the tried and tested magazine world, the fast-spreading radio networks or the still relatively novel talking pictures, anything that relieved the daily pressures and took one into a world of fantasy was all right by the public.

In the field of mass entertainment the Thirties, for publishing, were the decade of the Pulps. Along with the 'slicks'—the shiny paper magazines like Esquire, Colliers, Harpers, Life, Look, Time and McCalls—they filled the street-corner news-stands with a colourful array of penny-dreadful covers that has never been rivalled since. Top pulp writers like the great Walter Brown Gibson, creator of 'The Shadow', who typed on three machines in rotation and produced the equivalent of a 60,000 word novel every other week for more than ten years nonstop, filled the mass mind with such glorious titles as 'G-8 and His Battle Aces', 'Black Mask', 'The Mysterious Wu Fang', 'Thrilling Wonder Stories', 'Amazing Stories', 'Black Book Detective', 'The Spider', 'Secret Agent X', 'Jungle Stories', 'Argosy', 'Lariat Story Magazine', 'Two-Gun Western' and the rest. Street and Smith, top pulp publishers, put out titles that covered everything from love stories to space monsters, taking in crime—from both sides of the fence—the Wild West and World Wars on the way. As the real life idols fell as fast as share-prices, the fantasy world of the pulps was irresistible. Even that true-life gangbuster, Edgar Hoover, wasn't averse to a flip through the pages of 'Black Book Detective' or 'Racketeer Stories' in his off-duty moments. In the Thirties, when pulps were at their height, their covers even boasted the NRA trademark, the Blue Eagle, proudly stating 'We Do Our Part'.

But even the pulps, those action-packed easiest to read magazines, were soon to be outclassed by another media success—the radio—spreading across the country as fast as the big companies—NBC with its Red and Blue channels, CBS and the defunct MBS—could set up transmitters and man the local stations. At the flick of a switch and the twist of a dial every home could tune in to a new world of fantasy and a whole range of stars who made their names in the burgeoning medium. Radio serials, known as 'soap operas' from their early sponsorship by the detergent firm of Proctor and Gamble, grabbed regular audiences whose whole lifestyle was orientated to the daily dose of 'Our Gal Sunday', 'Today's Children', 'The Guiding Light', 'Just Plain Bill' and dozens of others. Many of them are still going, alongside their TV coun-

J. Edgar Hoover — what subconscious fear turned this humble man into the greatest crime-busting super-cop ever to turn a villain's legs to jelly? We shall never ever know — he took his secret to the grave.

terparts. Gertrude Berg, who played her own star character 'Molly Goldberg' in 'The Goldbergs', originated the mode, became a national figure and ended by taking her 'family' onto the Broadway stage.

The soaps were only a part of the massive armoury of day-long radio shows. "There are three things I shall never forget about America," said George Bernard Shaw. Apart from the Rocky mountains and the Statue of Liberty, GBS included a radio show: 'Amos 'n' Andy'. Today, the 'chocolate coloured coon' allusions of the show, in which the all-black characters were performed by two white actors Freeman Gosden and Charles Correll, are blatantly racist. But in the Thirties they wowed America from FDR downwards. With such support stars as 'Kingfish', the archetypal Harlem hustler, and 'Lightnin'', a clean-up man, 'Amos 'n' Andy' had America rolling around its firesides.

Apart from the comedy shows—Fibber McGee and Molly, Ozzie and Harriet, Edgar Bergen (father of Candice) and Charlie McCarthy his dummy—there was an earfull of daily listening that ranged from Walter Winchell's gossipy New York programme to Dale Carnegie urging the scared to 'Win Friends and Influence People'—even H. V. Kaltenborn, a radio-based Walter Cronkite of his age. On the serious side, Thirties' radio reached its apogee on October 30, 1938, when the Mercury Theatre On The Air broadcast through CBS their dramatised version of H. G. Wells' 'War of the Worlds'. Narrator Orson Welles, the young genius of the American Theatre of the time, and his cast put out a show that made the sort of hit no-one could ever have every imagined. All over the country listeners were left in no doubt that Martians, complete with death rays and space ships really *had* landed! In New Jersey, where the landings had supposedly taken place, the roads were filled with refugees from an imagined nightmare just up the road. Scarcely a month earlier in Europe, Britain's appeasing Prime Minister Neville Chamberlain had clambered down from a plane waving his celebrated piece of paper, the agreement with Adolf Hitler. Welles' radio refugees would be replaced all too soon by the real thing.

Of course of all the fantasy world in the media arsenal of the 1930s, nothing could compare with the fare provided by the real Dream Factory, Hollywood. Today's cineastes claim that little worthwhile has come out of Hollywood or the movie business in general since those glorious days, and reviewing the stars, the producers and directors and their movies, it's hard not to agree with them, however good subsequent movie making may occasionally be. Every truly great Hollywood performer was moulded into the all-powerful star system that ruled the movie capital's roost in the Thirties. The list of superstars is endless. Bette Davis in 'The Letter', Fred Astaire and Ginger Rogers in 'The Gay Divorcee', Dick Powell serenading Ruby Keeler in '42nd Street' (just one of the ex-West Point drill sergeant Busby Berkeley's swirling escapist fantasies), Clark Gable and Claudette Colbert in 'It Happened One Night', James Stewart, Katherine Hepburn and Cary Grant in 'The Philadelphia Story' and, not forgetting the monster's monster, King Kong.

ABOVE: Big bands were big business, and that meant Hollywood exploitation. Every studio had its swing movie, and all the top names trooped out to the Coast to get their moving pictures taken. The films suffered from third-rate plots and fourth-rate scripts. Only the music survived the cameras, and that was sometimes an uphill struggle. Glenn Miller's efforts, "Sun Valley Serenade" and "Orchestra Wives", were rated better than par. Maybe that was why he charged admission to the press previews. The critics may have griped, but the movie moguls were pleased.

ABOVE: Only the select were granted Hollywood's ultimate accolade, the all-star, full colour biopic. Goodman, the Dorseys and of course Glenn Miller. Jimmy Stewart played his usual farm boy next door, and June Allyson made the best of Helen Miller. Chummy MacGregor came in as official adviser and Stewart only mimed the trombone sections. For years to come, this epic of Fifties sentimentality would stand as the authorised version of Miller's life. "The Glenn Miller Story" confirmed his status. Miller, once a private memory had become a public myth.

Crime, inevitably, had pride of place, after love, in the movies. Even after the Hays Office (the movie moguls self-imposed censorship department which was established to pre-empt any governmental attempts to control them) and the Catholic bishops' League of Decency had 'cleaned up' the movies after 1934, the exploits of criminals ranked high in the popularity polls. Edward G. Robinson, James Cagney, Paul Muni and of course Humphrey Bogart elevated the hood to a cult figure. Maybe he did have to get his deserts in the end, but he had his fling. Commenting on the puritan, hypocritical restrictions of the Hays Office Herman Mankiewicz, writer with Welles of 'Citizen Kane' and brother of producer

Joseph Mankiewicz, put it succinctly: 'In a novel the hero can lay ten gals and marry a virgin at the finish. In a movie this is not allowed. The hero as well as the heroine has to be a virgin. The villain can lay anyone he wants, have as much fun as he likes getting rich and cheating the servants. But you have to shoot him in the end.'

Of course there were drawbacks to the Hollywood monolith. The versions of fantasy foisted on the public were usually far from the truth, as the sort of movies made around the big Swing bands proved. Glenn Miller's appearances in 'Orchestra Wives' and 'Sun Valley Serenade' give a very distorted view of big band life. Their nearest parallel are the movies made twenty years later to exploit the stardom of such rock musicians as Elvis Presley or Cliff Richard. The biopics made to honour the big band leaders, epitomised in Miller's posthumous tribute 'The Glenn Miller Story', were, inevitably, mawkish drivel.

But reality, in the Thirties just like at any other time, maintained its uncanny ability to put art to shame. Flash Gordon may have been pitting his wits against Ming the Merciless, and Dick Tracy possibly battling his way through every bizarre crook that Chester Gould could put in his way, but in America and in Europe events were rapidly coming to a head on the social and political fronts. Few people appreciated it at the time, but what were a few 'gangland slayings' compared with the Nazi concentration camps? Hitler or Mussolini had a better claim to the title of 'Public Enemy Number One than the quaintly nicknamed outlaws of the Mid-Western states or the big cities. America even threw up its own dictator, however mild he may have been compared with the excesses of Hitler or Stalin. Huey P. Long, Governor of Louisiana, known to his adoring public as 'The Kingfish', whose election anthem promised that 'Every man's a King', was America's version of the revolutionary one-man ruler. Outside his home state few had any time for the Kingfish's frank demagoguery. His appeal was based on a tract entitled 'Share Our Wealth' which preached Robin Hood-style economic reforms. This won over the people, but in practice Huey Long knew it was safer to soak the poor and cultivate the rich. He was convinced that Louisiana would carry him to the Presidency and even wrote an optimistic biography, 'My First Days in the White House'. In 1935 he was gunned down in the midst of his own supporters.

Every decade has its flavour, usually summed up in a few trite words. The Thirties, surely, were the Desperate Years. They started in economic chaos and ended with the world plunged into the second world war in a mere quarter of a century. Some would say that the first war had never ended, and after all, armed struggles are only a development of their economic background. Whether one had M. Claudel's champagne, or only the media surrogates of the radio, movie or magazine fantasy worlds, there was indeed little to do in between the crisis and the catastrophe but to enjoy oneself as best one could. The only real attempt to ward off the tide of fascism, the bitterly fought and tragically concluded Spanish Civil War, gave the West's young left-wingers a chance to practise their trench warfare and the Germans an opportunity to rehearse the Blitzkreig. It wasn't hard to see which technique came off best. Stripping away the escapism of the media, the Thirties are a bleak ten years. The joy and relief of the Twenties, however superficial it may have been, was brutally gutted by the Crash. From thereon in the progress towards War was obvious, even if no-one really wanted to admit it. The inconsistencies of the 1918 settlements had paved the way, but it took twenty years for the actual re-declaration of hostilities. In the meantime a desperate world waited out the political manoeuvrings. They read the pulps, they hero-worshipped the FBI or the criminals according to taste, they listened to the radio and went out to the movies. They had to do something. And there was something else that helped take their minds off the miserable facts. Another entertainment that put paid to the continual worry with a shot of happiness. If you didn't fancy the radio, and you'd seen all the movies and read all the magazines, there was always another escape. It wasn't quite as easy a fantasy, but after all it was open to everyone. It was young, it was revolutionary, you could bring it home or it made a great evening out: *it was Swing Music.*

CHAPTER TWO

MILLER-SON OF MATTIE

HE WAS AS AMERICAN as Mom's Apple Pie. A Norman Rockwell child, tow-headed, clear-eyed. Later, at college, he would have the same clean, bland features that typified all those boys who danced their last dance in the clubs and halls 'somewhere in England', 'Moonlight' Serenade' still echoing against the throb of the planes on the long, perilous haul to Berlin, Hamburg, or the Ruhr.

An impeccable Mid-West background, his childhood was a universe of small towns. Clarinda, Iowa, where Alton Glenn Miller was born, on March 1st, 1904; Tryon, Nebraska where Glenn, father Lewis Elmer Miller and mother Mattie Lou Cavender lived in a sod hut; North Platte, Nebraska; Grant City, Missouri; Fort Morgan, Colorado. Undistinguished homes for an undistinguished family. Elmer Miller—like sons Glenn, Deane and Herbert the elder Miller never used his first christian name—was no success story. Carpenter, school porter, homesteader . . . there were millions of Millers in that world of Main Street, of Babbitts and Boosters and 'the wrong side of the tracks'.

It was a world of little material joy, a dour struggle for survival when the American matriarch gripped hard to what little stability could be found. Mattie Lou played the organ in impromptu home worship, organised her three boys and the daughter Irene for what schooling they could get in the early wandering years, inculcated them with the simple black and white credos of Protestant, Mid-Western America. The slogans of self improvement, 'If you're gonna be good, be doggone good' and the endless demands that one aimed only for excellence, for perfection. Thirty years later Miller refused to play the instrument he loved because others were nearer that perfection he was convinced he could never really achieve.

Remember that Apple Pie. *Mom's*. Elmer fades quickly out of the Glenn Miller story. Mattie Lou steeled herself for the struggle and marked her boy for life. All those ethical encouragements, that neat assumption that you were either good/successful or bad/failed. The boyhood heroes: Horatio Alger and Teddy Roosevelt. One the epitome of the self-made man, his massive output of books promising that coveted *success* to every devotee of the American Dream; and the other the personification of that Dream, leading his 'Rough Riders' to show the world that the Manifest Destiny would be, indeed was even then being achieved. Heroes for the hopeful, the poor, the 'little people' who would raise the standard of 'Middle America' a generation after Miller vanished and another crop of their sons were offered up as America's cannon-fodder.

But if Mom held the psychic whip hand, then Paw had his role to play in the Mid-West rags to riches tale. The All-American boy, Glenn played baseball, basketball and football and his first ambition was a spot on a pro Baseball outfit. At highschool he played 'end' on the football team and pictures show him foursquare to the camera, his slim frame bulked out by the archaic padding of the era. Maybe he might have made the big leagues, certainly half the big bands seemed to worship the baseball diamond when they weren't up on their own bandstands. No-one will know. Around 1912 Paw Miller found a job as foreman for the Union Pacific Rail Road on a group of their bridges. It meant money; more, no doubt, than a janitor or a journeyman carpenter could pick up. One day he brought young Glenn a present—a mandolin. In 1915, eleven years old, Glenn traded his mandolin for a horn. The die had been cast. From now on, music would be young Miller's number one fascination. Through High School at Fort Morgan and a short college career at the University of Colorado, Glenn Miller nurtured his passion and his ability. Naturally, he had learned his lesson well, he had to be the best.

Alton Glenn Miller graduated from Fort Morgan High School in the Class of 1921. Looking along his class lists it's easy to see those small town kids. No Jews, Italians or similar exotics. The odd German, maybe a Swede, but mainly solid Farnsworths, Crouches, Bakers, Leonards and Johnstons. The very backbone of the American way. Like Mattie Lou the mothers joined the Women's Christian Temperance Union, waging righteous war on the demon alcohol—like Glenn the kids absorbed all those high minded ideals, the repression and the reticence. How many, one wonders, forgot their temperance twenty years later and like Glenn, proved savage, aggressive drunks when the once forbidden liquor took over those well turned out, straight laced minds.

Glenn's high school career, like his collegiate year, proved nothing exceptional. He did occasional factory jobs, rather more soda-

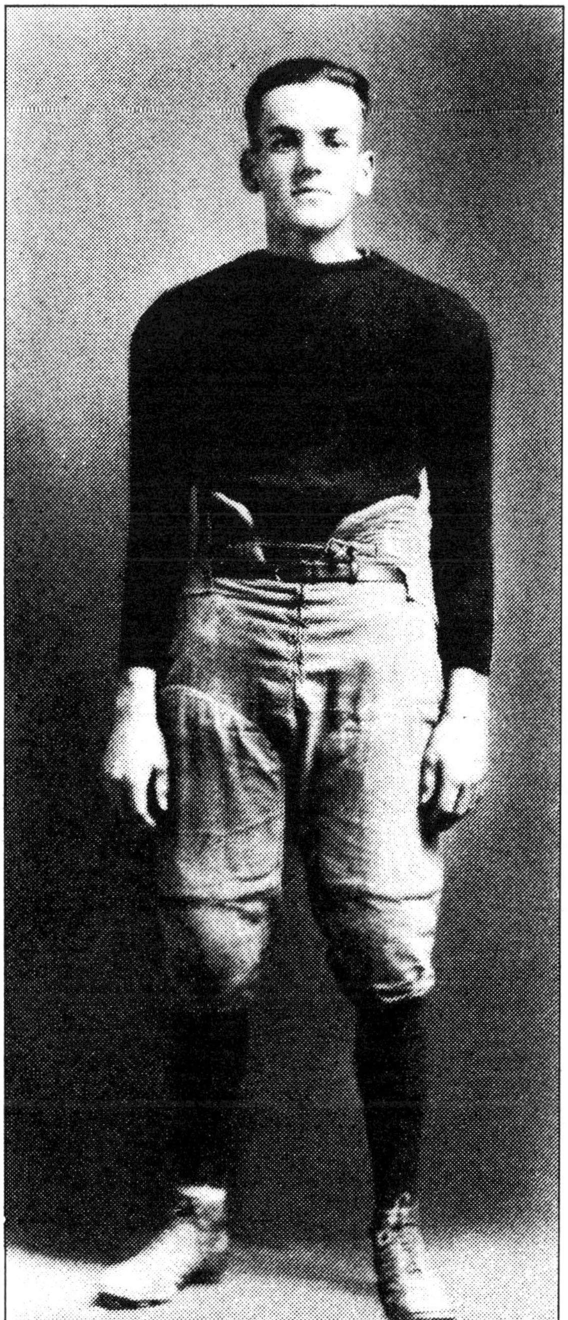

ABOVE: Teenaged Glenn Miller worked out for the High School gridiron squad but like so many fledgling swing stars, his main sport was baseball. If Elmer Miller hadn't bought him his first instrument, maybe young Glenn would have diverted his ambitions towards the baseball diamond and not the bandstand. In the event, sporting prowess gave way to greater things. *FACING PAGE:* Without doubt the kid's number one influence remained his Mother, Mattie. She played the organ, taught her boys the Protestant ethic, and campaigned for Prohibition. Later, a grateful son set her up in a New York apartment and showed her off at his sell - out gigs. Mattie's Mid - West philosophies went on to create a major talent, and Glenn was never to escape her simple sloganeering. 'If you're gonna be good,' she assured him, 'be doggone good.' Warts and all, he was.

jerking and newspaper delivery—the traditional teenage occupations to scrape up those extra funds. His trombone playing was nothing out of the ordinary either. Jack Mossberger, a local Fort Morgan store owner who also ran the local combo, had given him the trombone. While Miller practised assiduously, there weren't any apparent clues as yet as to the

ABOVE: **Don't believe everything you see at the movies. Miller and Chummy MacGregor didn't exactly spend all their youth in and out of pawn shops, no matter how much time Jimmy Stewart spent hicking his trombone. But they *are* on their way to join Ben Pollack.**

future. He was a middle of the road kid in a middle of the road world. Of course there was one thing that cut him out of the ruck: living up to all those Protestant myths meant hard work. It also meant something else: ambition.

It was his musical ambition, of course, that effectively ended his education at the University of Colorado before it had begun. There were classes in English, History, Personal Hygiene and the rest and Miller duly attended them. He can't have been interested, as his mediocre grades, repeats of his school reports which featured mainly 'C' grades, were to prove. But what did classes matter when there in college was a living, breathing example of Glenn's real interest: music? If Glenn cut classes for the meagre three quarters of the academic year he attended U.C. then it wasn't because he was avoiding *all* his lessons. Almost from the day he arrived, the fledgling trombonist made his way into the ranks of Holly Moyer's Band, the campus favourites. Moyer's wasn't the first band Miller had tried out for after school. On the very day of his graduation in 1920 it wasn't Glenn who donned cap and gown to step up and receive his high school diploma. No, He was in Laramie, Wyoming looking for a trombone gig that didn't materialise. Back in Fort Morgan, with convenient symbolism, it was Mattie Lou Miller who collected the token tribute to Miller's lackadaisical schooldays.

Based around the university's Sigma Nu fraternity, the Moyer band played both on and off the campus and like many of the college bands that emerged across the Mid- and South-West in the early Twenties, they proved reasonably successful. The appeals of music over work are shown simply in Miller's final assessments when he left college in Autumn 1923. After a mere eight months in college Miller's personal course completion managed 3 out of 16 semesters and only 36 out of 186 graduating marks. Mattie Lou wouldn't be turning up for anything at this stage of Glenn's education. Not unless, of course, she happended to be a jazz fan.

The Moyer band proved a useful launching pad for Miller. In the first place it obviously helped him progress in his trombone playing. And, as the future would prove, he made his tentative steps into a career in which he excelled to an extent which rivalled any of his big band contemporaries: arranging. Perhaps his trombone playing never did make the heights of, say, Tommy Dorsey, but his arranging, for Dorsey among others, left little to be desired in the way of excellence.

With Moyer Glenn toured a couple of times around Wyoming in 1923 and in September of that year he tried for a place in another, even more popular college outfit: Jimmy Joy's Band, based on the young players of the University of Texas. In the event Glenn just wasn't up to scratch. But the experience would pay off later, even though in his disappointment Glenn probably didn't realise it at the time. Fronting the band as singer was one Smith Ballew, a super-smooth example of film-star looks with a romantically crooning voice to match. When Smith Ballew led his own band a few years later, among his sidemen was Glenn Miller. Whatever may have come of Miller's attempt to grab a slot with Jimmy Joy (who was actually called Jimmy Mahoney), it paid off in the long run.

When Glenn dropped out of class for the last time in September 1923 and put paid once and for all to his academic life, he didn't have to quit the Moyer Band as well. He stayed on with them for a while, then joined another relatively unknown setup, Tom Watkins' Band. More touring of the South-West followed and then Miller arrived in Los Angeles, where he joined Max Fischer's band who played in the Forum Theatre. It was lacklustre work, but Miller, always a good technical musician if not actually an inspired solo performer, did his undemanding job well enough. But it didn't seem to point any shining light towords a golden future. No matter. If Elmer Miller's goodtime gift had set his son on the way to fame back in 1912, then another push on the road to stardom was there right on schedule in 1925.

Years later, on one of those questionnaires so beloved by music writers and the fans that read them, Glenn Miller summed up that forwards thrust succinctly: 'The break of fortune that shaped my career: the interest that Ben Pollack showed in me when he hired me to play and arrange for his band.'

Families flocked to the Big Bands. Bing's kid brother Bob Crosby led a dixieland lineup that recycled Ben Pollack's stars. Miller's trombone paid its dues for a while.

CHAPTER THREE

TROMBONIST ON A TREADMILL

IN EVERY ERA and in every variety of enterprise, there's always someone or something to which all the ambitious will look. For the aspiring young jazz musicians of the 1920s, the white ones anyway, the current apogee of high-class musicianship sat enthroned on the bandstands occupied by the Ben Pollack Band. Along with the Red Nichols and Miff Mole outfits, Pollack's Band represented the epitome of classy playing in jazz men's eyes. Apart from the amazing lineup of embryo stars—Miller himself, Benny Goodman, Jack Teagarden, Charlie Spivak and the nucleus of the future Bob Crosby Band among many other top names to be—the main appeal of Pollack was that his lineup was responsible for the best of the 'hot' jazz creations of the late twenties.

Black musicians like Ellington and Fletcher Henderson may have been playing 'hot' jazz for years, but among white bands, there was still something faintly exotic about this music which relied more on the hard-edged afro-american rhythms of the blacks than on the essentially 'sweet' sound of most popular dance music of the late twenties, as exemplified by Paul Whiteman. It was inevitable that hopeful young musicians would look towards this new and exciting sound in an effort to realise their own musical aims. Fortunately for them Ben Pollack wasn't slow to pick up on the talents available to him. Benny Goodman was hired at the age of sixteen and turned up to play still wearing short pants! Pollack did persuade him to get a pair of long trousers for his appearances on the stand. And in the wake of Goodman came other ambitious hopefuls. With Pollack's punchy drumming to set the style, they all helped make his band an exemplar for everyone who wanted a little more out of their music than the 'sweet' combos were providing.

Naturally Pollack's wasn't completely free of commercial taints. For a start its leader unfortunately fancied his own voice and made a few appalling cuts featuring his own vocals. He should have stuck to the sticks. Pollack also had another trait which can't have exactly delighted his more discerning fans. Many of his records would end with the leader signing off with an ingratiating 'May it please you, Ben Pollack.' But it was a time like any other: Pollack's abilities and the potential of his musicians were one thing; the demands of the record companies and the public they played for were something else. Hot jazz was fine for the connoisseurs, but if you wanted to keep eating, you had to mix it in with plenty of the old corn. An unfortunate fashion in the twenties, for the banal style of burlesque musicians, which seemed to appeal to many recording directors, meant that for every hot number, the Pollack Band had to throw in some clichéd horror.

It was with this need to quit the commercial side of the band in mind that many of Pollack's musicians went out and produced records under other names and for a variety of labels. Pollack never really approved of this and his musicians knew it. They called themselves 'Ben's Bad Boys' but didn't stop going off to the unofficial recording sessions. In the same vein, Pollack may have discovered an enormous amount of outstanding musicians, but he was never really able to hold on to them. He often complained that other leaders cannibalised his band, and there was no doubt that his discoveries did move on, often to set up their own bands. His band broke up in 1934, when the bulk of the remaining musicians went to form the basis of Bob Crosby's swing unit, but Pollack himself didn't give up the big band business for another eight years. In 1942 he broke up his last major band and went on the road with a small combo backing, of all people, Chico Marx! Through the fifties and sixties he ran a variety of West Coast clubs and finally committed suicide in June 1971, penniless and depressed.

What with his signing off recordings, his acceptance of a large amount of commercial influence and his inability to hang on to the stars he discovered, a retrospective on Pollack may not give him the acclaim he deserves. An uneasy fusion of progressive and functional music, the Pollack output was nothing compared to the sound the great black leaders were putting together by the end of the twenties. Still, it would be absurd to underestimate the importance of Ben Pollack. His was undoubtedly one of the few white bands of that era willing to experiment in a music influenced more by jazz than by popular dance music. His stars may have quit, but they had still come to him in the first place.

Glenn Miller, who stayed with the band from 1925 to 1928, was certainly one of those young stars in the making who was overjoyed

Miller, like all the rest, worked around the 'hot' outfits. Red Nichols and Miff Mole (*FACING PAGE*) epitomised New York's finest white playing. But the big break came on Ben Pollack's bandstand (*ABOVE*). Jack Teagarden (*BELOW*) had a talent which, in terms of technique and originality, far outstripped that of Miller.

ABOVE: Kay Weber was Bob Crosby's first canary. There would be many more, including Doris Day, Gloria De Haven and Kay Starr. Arrangers Henry Mancini and Nelson Riddle also came and went with Crosby. Red Nichols (*BELOW*) had some personnel changes himself.

by a chance to work with the great Pollack. However inaccurate the 'Glenn Miller Story' may be in its detail, it makes no mistake in underlying just how vital the Pollack slot was to the young trombonist even though his stint with the band was more important for his arranging than for his musicianship. In the late twenties Miller was still learning the arranging skills that would finally prove his greatest contribution to the sound of the swing era. He listened constantly to other bands, both on stage and on record, and used the styles he liked. The melodious strings of the Roger Wolfe Kahn Orchestra made their way onto Pollack's second 78 'Deed I Do', which was arranged by Miller for its 1926 recording by RCA Victor.

Miller's work as an arranger for Pollack was mainly on the commercial side of the fence. Fud Livingston, later an arranger for Jimmy Dorsey, was responsible for the jazz music. That didn't mean that Miller himself wasn't trying for a more exciting sound. His idol Miff Mole, who stood at the peak of the 'New York' style of jazz that dominated the late twenties, set the standards that the young trombonist aspired to. Unfortunately for Miller, these standards were quite simply too high for him to equal. In the years to come friendly critics went so far as to compare Miller's playing on some solo pieces with that of the great Miff Mole, but on the whole the leader to be was already showing that his arranging abilities were a far stronger suit than his playing.

Playing or arranging notwithstanding, the years Miller spent with Ben Pollack were certainly vital ones for him. And for the band as a whole they represented some of their greatest output. Tours of the South, of the West and across most of the country met with great popular success. Steady residencies at Chicago's Rendezvous and Blackhawk nightclubs, where gangland bootleg liquor arrived in teacups and its profits went to pay the musicians, kept packing in the patrons. It was an exciting time for Miller, still only in his early twenties. All the gaudy glamour of the Prohibition era, brought to its excessive heights in the wide-open city of Chicago, lying secure in Al Capone's greedy palm, surrounded his life with the band. How such degeneracy affected his mid-West conscience, still imbued with the milk of mother's rectitude, is unknown, but it's around this time that stories of Glenn's own interest in the bottle start to appear. No-one's agreed on the sort of drunk he was, but enough tales exist of his savage, destructive temper when liquored up to give some substance to his hard-drinking image. It was the breaking out that every young man, newly free from parental restraint, inevitably undergoes. But for Miller, whose restraints had been aggressively puritan in the first place, the explosion was all the more violent.

His inability to reach the really major heights of trombone-playing can't have helped either. Arranging was one thing; it was a skill he was gradually mastering and the contribution his work made to Pollack's band must not be underestimated. But for an ambitious young man like Glenn Miller, with all those maternal slogans of excellence pumped firmly onto his brain, playing must have mattered intensely. With such talents as Benny Goodman, Jimmy McPartland and the rest showing just what could be done with their instruments, it must have galled Miller to find that their perfection was somehow eluding him. Always a perfectionist, Glenn Miller was unable to find that demanding standard in the one thing nearest to his own heart—playing the trombone.

When he quit Pollack in 1928 it was this failure to reach the level of the toplining musicians that was behind his exit. No-one actually sacked him. Pollack didn't come out and condemn his abilities, and indeed his arranging was a mainstay of the Pollack appeal, but in his eyes it was his playing that finished his career with the Pollack band. One night in the late spring of 1928 Pollack number two man Gil Rodin, who was later to help Bob Crosby take over the nucleus of the Pollack band after its 1934 breakup, went over to a jam session in New York's Louisiana Apartments. There he heard a trombonist who quite simply blew his mind. Playing without a bell portion of the horn, Jack Teagarden was blowing straight through the slide into a glass. The sounds he produced were unlike anything Rodin, or any other of the Pollack musicians sitting in on the session had ever heard. It was musical love at first sight.

Jack Teagarden was one of the outstanding jazz trombonists of that or any other time. His 'glass-blowing' expertise may have wowed the Pollack bandsmen, but his playing was generally well-known to all jazz fans long before 1928. Ironically, while Teagarden's excellence endeared him to musicians and fans alike, and his solo work made for standout performances from every band he worked with, he was never really lucky in the leaders for whom he worked. His personal style was dramatic and idiosyncratic, but with both Paul Whiteman, with whom he stayed for five years, and Ben Pollack, for whom he put in another five, he found that what *they* wanted from him was all too often miles away from what he wanted to give. The misnamed 'King of Jazz' was always far too commercial for Teagarden's tastes, although he was bound to him under his five-year contract, and even Pollack, whose reputation comes mainly from his pioneering efforts in jazz playing, had too many popular records to be made for Teagarden's tastes.

His standout solos for Pollack on 'Sentimental Baby' and 'My Kinda Love'—both recorded with Benny Goodman on clarinet—can't disguise the fact that Pollack, like Whiteman before him, squandered the talent that Teagarden was offering. As a final irony Jack Teagarden's next leader, himself, proved as big a mistake as his predecessors. Only this time the causes were different. His musical abilities were given free rein, but Teagarden just wasn't cut out to be an organising businessman of the sort who made it really big in the Swing Era. It didn't help that his band was working through the war years either. From 1939-46 Teagarden struggled against the conscription of his musicians and against the administrative problems caused by an inevitably high turnover of the band. In 1946 he joined the mass of leaders who disbanded in a mere four weeks of Spring.

Had Teagarden been an expert of some instrument other than the trombone, it may be that Glenn Miller's career with the Pollack Band would have continued a while longer. Perhaps Goodman or McPartland might have

Blacks and whites didn't mix. Not on the street and certainly nowhere near the bandstand. But every rule needed its exception. Miller may have thought little of his talents, but one of the first mixed race line-ups were happy to have him along. Eddie Condon (*ABOVE LEFT*) and Pee Wee Russell (*ABOVE CENTRE*) joined Coleman Hawkins (*ABOVE RIGHT*, with Thelma Carpenter) to make up the black side of the 'Mound City Blues Blowers'. Miller and other white stars kept up the Caucasian end. Hawkins was biggest of the three. Ex-Fletcher Henderson, his tenor sax had the young Charlie Barnet in ecstasies. Later he worked for Lionel Hampton. Miller always backed Tex Beneke's playing against Hawkins', but there weren't many takers.

quit to leave room for the talented new boy. As it was, Teagarden's brilliance was highlighted disastrously by Miller's own failings. Gil Rodin has since claimed that even as he asked Teagarden to join the band he still had vague hopes that Miller could stay on and play with him, but to a soul so acutely sensitive to his own deficiencies as Miller's, there was never a chance. The band was booked for a gig in Atlantic City, but Miller told Pollack that he wouldn't be leaving with them. No doubt bitterly disappointed, he managed to make a graceful exit from a situation that he could do nothing about. Claiming, rightly, that he had been offered a job by Paul Ash to write arrangements for the pit orchestra of New York's Paramount Theatre, he made his excuses and quit Ben Pollack.

The remainder of 1928 was bleak for Miller. The one high spot was his marriage to his college sweetheart Helen Burger. The hometown paper in Boulder, Colorado, called him 'the highest paid trombone player in the United States' but that star billing didn't quite match up to reality. Like the comedians who bridged the gaps between strippers in the burleque shows, the Paramount pit musicians were there merely to fill in between movies. Ash's arranging jobs hardly gave Miller the scope and direction he was looking for. There was money, but that wasn't enough.

As the twenties wound to a close, and the boom years teetered perilously towards the Crash of 1929 and the Depression beyond, Glenn Miller's own fortunes began to look unpleasantly shaky. He was working, but however good the gigs he picked up might be, he was always fated to run up against some superior trombonist. In early 1929 he cut twelve sides with the Dorsey Brothers Orchestra, but his feelings of insecurity weren't helped when he heard the masterly musicianship of featured trombonists like Tommy Dorsey and, inevitably, Jack Teagarden, imported for the session. Still, it would be wrong to dismiss Miller as a second rate musician. The simple fact that he was invited onto so many sessions, where top musicians like Goodman, drummer Gene Krupa, the Dorseys and others were also playing, shows that whatever his personal problems with his instrument, his peers had given him a good reputation. In November 1929, barely a month after Wall Street had collapsed and taken the world's economy with it, Miller featured in a breakthrough session. Under the name of the Mound City Blue Blowers, such talents as Miller, Krupa, Eddie Condon, Pee Wee Russell and Coleman Hawkins cut a number of tracks. For the very first time jazz had been recorded by a band, however temporary, which included both blacks and whites. If Miller thought he was just an also-ran that milestone session should have convinced him that he was up there with the men who mattered.

While the Depression savaged the recording industry, its effect was less destructive on the bands themselves, although quality certainly suffered. Just as Hollywood turned its energies towards an orgy of escapism, anything to help a miserable nation forget its financial woes, so did the music business concentrate on good time sounds. The trend towards 'hot' jazz that had been gradually eroding the dominance of 'sweet' music in the late twenties ground to a speedy halt. Everyone had to be cheered up. There was no time for the tortured rhythms and expressive solo performances of the real jazz. The mood was sweet, sickly sweet and while the 'hot' musicians kept on working, it was more likely than not on gigs that failed to reflect the sort of music they actually wanted to play. Not until 1935, six years after the Crash, did Swing break through and put paid to the sweetly escapist music once and for all.

The underlying theme of at least half the 'Glenn Miller Story' is the star's undying search for his 'sound'. It would be more accurate to stress Miller's search, like that of his fellow musicians, for work. Fortunately for him the reputation he had built up before 1929 served him in good stead during its worst years. With his new wife he lived in an apartment in 29th Street in Astoria, Queens and in common with other musicians he picked up his money from a variety of session work. In 1930 his main employer was Red Nichols, the veteran who had often worked with Miller's idol, Miff Mole. The bands Nichols and Mole put together, under such names as 'Red and Miff's Stompers', 'the Charleston Chasers' and 'the Red Heads' were some of the best exponents of the hot jazz tradition. Nichols has been awarded the dubious accolade of a Hollywood biography on film, and Danny Kaye portrayed the leader in 'The Five Pennies', the name of his best-known unit. The 'Pennies', in common with many of their contemporaries, were a flexible lineup who rarely limited themselves to a mere five musicians. Along with Glenn Miller they played for George Gershwin's musical 'Girl Crazy' and another Broadway hit, 'Strike Up The Band'. Such stars as Goodman and Krupa were recruited alongside Miller for these pick-up pit orchestras. Indeed, in 1931, Miller cut no less than 18 sides with Goodman, but not as featured trombonist. True to form, that coveted spot fell to Jack Teagarden.

Looking at the Depression era, it is very hard to keep an accurate track of any of the musicians who were destined for stardom in the Swing Era. No one seemed to play in the same band or turn up in the same recording studios for any consecutive length of time. The flexibility of all the lineups of that time gives the impression of a floating population of talented musicians working for a number of administrative figures who put together the various bands as, when and where they were required. The clubs and recording studios provided a countrywide musical melting pot in which every musician of worth could be found and appreciated according to taste. Following Glenn Miller has the same pitfalls as studying any of the other stars in the making. One can only take the main reference points and work from there.

After Nichols and the recordings with Goodman, Miller's next leader was Smith Ballew, the same debonair figure who had fronted Jimmy Joy's college combo ten years earlier. Ballew was forming his own band now and he suggested to Miller that he should join him as leader. He would play his trombone, help rehearse the band and take care of the arranging – all for $250 a week and 50% of everything over $1,000 for the week's gigs. Nichols had paid Miller $125 a week, some way above the official union scale of $80; but this was an excellent chance. Yet the financial benefits of working with Ballew were more than outweighed by the musical drawbacks. The band was never really a cohesive unit, eternally hovering just on the point of collapse. Miller

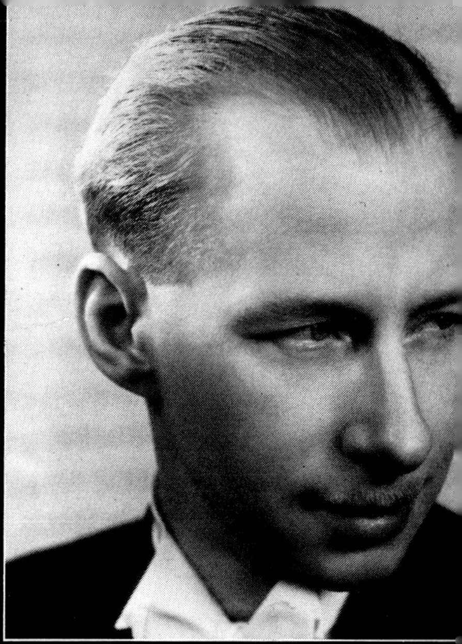

Hollywood had no mercy, but at least the 'Fabulous Dorseys' starred the brothers themselves (*ABOVE LEFT*). Actress Janet Blair was the real thing too. As Janet Lafferty she'd been hired by Hal Kemp for vocals. Her new name apparently helped with projection. Ray Noble (*ABOVE RIGHT*) lost his British lineup, but ex-Dorsey Brothers arranger Glenn Miller filled the gaps.

wanted one thing from the musicians while Ballew was on an entirely different track. They worked sporadically until 1933, with gigs in New York, New Orleans, St. Paul, Pittsburgh and finally Denver. Unhappy with a band that failed to meet his exacting standards Miller became more and more of a martinet. Everyone who remembers him in this era has pictured a severe, uptight, standoffish figure. When the band broke up and Miller moved on, there were few regrets on either side.

Yet it is impossible not to sympathise with Glenn Miller. He knew more and more what he wanted, how he wanted to run a band and the fact that his background experience and definite abilities made him perfectly capable of putting his plans into action. Whether, of course, they would be successful was something he couldn't predict. As the 1930s moved on, he was gradually moving nearer the autonomy that his character and his hopes were making more and more necessary, but it was still not time for him to branch out, even after his departure from the Ballew Orchestra.

In 1934 Miller moved on to working for the Dorsey Brothers Orchestra. A far more professional and talented band than Ballew's, featuring no less a figure than Bing Crosby as their singer, the Dorsey Brothers gave Miller opportunities for further development as an arranger. One of three trombones in the band, he could never rival the skills of Tommy Dorsey, but his work arranging for Crosby stood him in good stead. Working for the band was less rewarding. The Dorsey Brothers style encouraged spontaneous creativity, along the lines of the better black units, rather than the strictly rehearsed arrangements Miller was putting together. The continual feuding between Tommy and Jimmy Dorsey didn't improve matters either. As the band's active but untitled musical director, Miller found himself caught between the fighting brothers. He didn't need the strain. Apart from anything else his income that year had dropped to little over three thousand dollars, less than half what he'd been making with Red Nichols and his session work. Frustrated once more, Miller quit the Dorsey Brothers.

In 1935 Miller found himself once more as the token leader of another man's musicians. Ray Noble, the star English bandleader, had been invited to the States, but Musicians Union rules made it impossible for him to bring his orchestra across the Atlantic. Rockwell-O'Keefe, the Dorsey Brothers' bookers, asked Miller to help out. He was to assemble a band for Noble and work with him on the jazz arranging while Noble stuck to the ballads which had been his speciality and which were interpreted to great acclaim by his South African singer Al Bowlly.

Once again it was the old story. Noble vanished temporarily to Hollywood for some movie scoring work. Back in New York Miller picked up his musicians, formed the band and whipped them into shape with his usual hard-line efficiency. He set one milestone by setting

ABOVE: South African Al Bowlly was 'Moonlight Serenade's' first crooner – it wasn't titled when he heard it. The Dorsey Brothers' Band set for a dive (*RIGHT*). At least Miller's at the top.

a style in rehearsals: never before had a band been paid for its playing off the stand. But Miller's perfectionist demands kept them long hours in the rehearsal room, and he probably knew all too well that payment was the best way of averting a rebellion. Working for Noble did bring Miller's finances back to par – he earned over $7,500 in 1935, but when the nominal leader returned from Hollywood there was soon a sharp split between the two articulate and talented men. Miller chafed under the bit as usual. And as usual he made the inevitable decision: he quit. Before he left, however, his work with Noble did produce one very important piece of work. 'Now I Lay Me Down To Sleep' was the title of a melodic, moving piece Miller scored and arranged for the band. Later it would be retitled: 'Moonlight Serenade' would prove the most undying memorial to Miller's talent the world would ever know.

When Miller left Noble, leading a wholesale rebellion of dissatisfied artists whose mass exodus crippled the band permanently, he had left his last supporting role. He had known what he wanted and where he was going for years now. If he continued working in a secondary capacity there would only be frustration and a prolonged sense of self-denial. He couldn't guarantee success, but he was determined to find out. In late 1936, a few months after quitting the frustrating security of Ray Noble's band, Glenn Miller started looking for his first musicians. The Glenn Miller Orchestra was on its way.

The first Miller band never had it easy. Maybe they didn't have to play with mudcaked trousers, whatever 'The Glenn Miller Story' showed, but their initial success all too quickly deteriorated into steady failure.

CHAPTER FOUR

SHARPS 'N' FLATS

IF THEIR LEADER'S pedigree meant anything at all, then things looked very good for the brand new Glenn Miller Orchestra. There wasn't a swing leader worthy of the name with whom Miller hadn't played, whether on stage or in the studio, or for whose band he hadn't penned one of his own special arrangements. Benny Goodman, both the Dorseys, Bob Crosby, Red Nichols; not to mention some of the black bands who were getting a second crack at fame as the gospel of swing which they had written a decade before was being spread by white bands. As Goodman became the 'King of Swing', and Tommy Dorsey its 'Sentimental Gentleman', it seemed as if some honorific title was just waiting for Glenn Miller to pick it up. With his background and the reputation he had earned, fame, surely, was just there for the asking.

Almost as soon as he had quit the Ray Noble band in early 1936, Miller set out to recruit his own band. To keep himself financially secure he played radio dates with Vincent Lopez' Band and Freddy Rich's Orchestra—the former of which employed Miller's future songbird Marion Hutton's sister Betty as their vocalist—but he made it clear to bookers and record studios that from now on any band for whom Glenn Miller worked would have to be his own personal lineup. It was a gamble, but Miller had been taking the back seat for too long now. 'The Glenn Miller Story' paints a picture of his early 1930s career as a succession of struggles for little, unrewarding jobs. The era was certainly a struggle for Glenn Miller, but money, after the disastrous year with the Dorsey Brothers, had been only a minor problem. The real difficulties came from his increasing frustration with the work he had to do and the status he received for doing it. Great talent, and Miller was certainly that, even if his actual playing wasn't quite out on the front line, never could stand that level of frustration for long. Especially when the talent is harnessed to such an adamant perfectionist as Miller was. It is surprising that he lasted as a second in command for as long as he did. Benny Goodman had been dragging ecstatic fans dancing into the aisles all over America ever since his shattering success at the Palomar Ballroom in Los Angeles as early as 1935, when Miller was still working with Ray Noble. The Dorseys, divided and working their own ways, were capitalising on their own talents, and every week the list of swing bands increased. Yet where was Miller, one of the leading figures in the bands for already at least a decade? Still making the rounds. Of all the topline veterans, Miller was one of the last to join the ranks of swing leaders.

The last months of 1936 found Miller hard at work looking for bright young talents to play in his new band. It can't have taken his musicians long to realise that they'd consigned themselves into the hands of a real martinet. Discipline was always at the forefront of Glenn Miller's band leadership. The less strictly led outfits might work for some people, but for him there was only one way—his way. Up in the unpretentious Haven Studios on W.54th St. he rehearsed them tirelessly, never stopping until he had obtained *exactly* the sound he wanted. Of course he set his boys a good example throughout. He had made it clear that the sort of musicians he was after would have to have more than mere musical talent, they were to epitomise the clean-cut, clean-living All-American Boys. Just like America's own radio star All-American Jack Armstrong, sponsored by Wheaties, they shouldn't betray the good boys' code. For his part Miller cut out his own besetting vice—the bottle. While he led bands the "mean drunk . . . straight out of Central Casting" became a regular sobersides.

In all fairness, Glenn Miller's autocratic style had its points. While on the one hand it never gave free rein to standout talents in the way that a Jimmy Dorsey or a Count Basie was always happy to do, it certainly ended up paying dividends. As far as cutting out the drinking was concerned, he wasn't being stupid either. It didn't take much intelligence to check out the disastrous collapse of such starry careers as those of Bix Beiderbecke or Bunny Berigan, and see that if you couldn't handle drink, it was best to avoid it. Mattie Lou's forays with the WCTU had borne fruit, albeit twenty years later than she'd made them. But drinking apart, the most cursory glance at the careers of the great swing bands and their leaders makes one thing obvious: discipline really counted. The big bands, with their mass of musicians, presented problems in terms of logistics, apart from anything else, that could only be dealt with by efficiency and solid leadership. Miller may have proved too much of an autocrat in some areas, the later case of his dismissal of singer Ray Eberle stands as an obvious example, but his hardlining certainly paid off.

ABOVE: **Uptight Tommy Dorsey. Only his sound gave him his 'Sentimental Gentleman' title. The rest was much more practical.**

Miller trekked his way around the bands like every other young hopeful of the era. Whether he joined the likes of Benny Goodman (*FACING PAGE*) in the studios, or boosted yet another version of Red Nicholls' (*ABOVE*) 'Five Pennies', Miller kept paying his dues.

In the late Spring of 1937 Miller's Orchestra played their first public gig at the Hotel New Yorker in New York. It was only a fill-in for one night but Seymour Weiss of New Orleans' Roosevelt Hotel was passing through and liked what he heard. They moved into the Roosevelt's Blue Room in June for a two week residency. They left on August 25th, ten record-breaking nonstop weeks behind them. The previous best stay at the Roosevelt had been five weeks, so Miller and his boys felt justifiably proud. Indeed, their pride must have increased since March 1937, a mere month before Weiss heard them at the New Yorker, when a recording date at Decca had so worried Miller that he supplemented his inexperienced musicians with some old friends. Veterans like Charlie Spivak, Sterling Bose and Howard Smith helped flesh out the five cuts the band laid down at the session.

The Blue Room residency had been a wonderful start for the band, but all too soon it turned out to be no more than a honeymoon for Miller's lineup. He employed two new musicians, Irving 'Fazola' Prestopnik and Bob Price, for the clarinet and number one trumpet slots. If he'd still been after his all-American boys, he couldn't have picked a less likely duo, especially the jolly, overweight Fazola. Fazola's clarinet was undoubtedly one of the greatest renditions of that instrument around, but his genius was balanced by his taste for a lifestyle well removed from Miller's restricted ideas. He drank and experimented with marijuana—an event less common than sensational 'jazz movies' have led audiences to believe. On the one hand his clarinet proficiency must have helped Miller develop his own experimental uses of the clarinet, culminating in the predominant use he made of it

ABOVE: **Rock festivals, thirties-style! Benny Goodman and the band wow vacationing kids. Maybe the guys did look a bit on the strange side and on or off the stage it was strictly short-back-and-sides. The wire netting was the same as ever.**

ABOVE: **All-time trombone star Jack Teagarden just blew them all off stage. Trouble was, super-talented Teagarden should have stayed a soloist. Big band bosses needed more than creativity to keep the boys in line. The business was never Jack's long suit.**

in his arranging, but Fazola's excesses gradually worked their way through to the rest of the band. Perhaps, as some writers allege, he actually 'corrupted' the young Jack Armstrongs. More likely the depressingly accelerated downtrend in the band's fortunes helped turn everyone, clean-cut or not, towards some way of drowning their sorrows.

The worries Miller had made obvious when he hired his old friends for the March recordings were beginning to recur. His boys, however well rehearsed, *were* inexperienced and it began to show, despite the record run in New Orleans. They had managed some six sides in the two hour session back in March, but another session arranged for December 1937 took five tortuous hours to cut a mere couple of tracks. Miller was a perfectionist, but better musicians would never have taken so long for so little output.

By the end of the year the fate of the once-promising Glenn Miller Orchestra was nothing if not depressing. Minimal recording output to one side, their short gigs around the country—Dallas and Minneapolis among other cities—showed a declining trend. Audiences may have wanted swing, but so far the brand that Miller was putting out wasn't the sort they were after. The band's morale slipped lower in conjunction with their poor performances. Miller himself lost heart as they trailed from one unsuccessful gig to another. it didn't help, of course, that his own perfectionist attitudes undermined his faith in himself. On the one hand he was sure that he, and he alone, was capable of forming the band that he wanted, but on the other he was unable to make himself into a star leader in the way other

'Cheery, Chubby Charlie Spivak', as the punters called him, went the regular rounds before Glenn Miller set him up with a band. Like so many standout soloists, Spivak lost in individual style what he gained in all-round line-up.

swing names had managed. Goodman or the Dorseys, Artie Shaw or Duke Ellington were all capable of forming the whole style of the band around their own talents and personality. In time Miller's arranging would create a band that was as dependant on his particular abilities as Goodman's or Tommy Dorsey's were on their playing, but in late 1937 there was no sign of his coming stardom. Ever since Pollack had hired Jack Teagarden as a better trombonist back in 1927, Glenn Miller had created for himself a myth that he was a lousy trombonist. True, he wasn't the greatest. But the lists of infinitely lesser musicians, be they drummers, pianists, trumpeters or whatever, who were sufficiently confident to form bands around their own playing shows that Miller was deluding himself sadly.

As winter took 1937 into 1938 the fortunes of the Glenn Miller Orchestra kept plummetting down. A series of soul-destroying one-nighters put paid to any hopes the band may have had of recovering and getting back to the success of the Roosevelt. On New Year's Eve they played a desultory set at the Valencia Ballroom in lowly York, Pennsylvania. It was all too much. Miller gave his band a final notice and after one last appearance in the Ritz Ballroom in Bridgeport, Connecticut the Glenn Miller Orchestra broke up. It's hard to imagine that anyone felt that sad about the collapse. The wound had festered long enough. A speedy amputation, however long and mistakenly it had been delayed, must have been the best bet.

For the leader, of course, the disbanding was appalling. While his musicians, used to the flexible lifestyle of the era, went off and found themselves jobs with other leaders, their late leader himself had no such solace. He did a few spots on Tommy Dorsey's regular Raleigh-Kool radio show and worked on an arrangement for Benny Goodman. Goodman rejected it as too pretty for his swinging musicians. It was a bitter pill. *Metronome* magazine columnist George T. Simon who latterly became Glenn Miller's leading biographer, had headed a column in March 1937 'The Country's Newest Coming Band?!' and talked of 'a pretty easy climb to the top.' Now, barely twelve months later, it looked as if the 'coming' band had been and swiftly gone.

Working his passage, as second in command or musical director to the best of his contemporaries had left Miller with one set of frustrations. He knew what he wanted; he had to find out how *he* would make out as a band leader in his own right. Now, with the experiment brought to a miserable conclusion, he had a whole new set. He had tried, and he had most undeniably failed. It was hardly calculated to brighten the wintry days.

But Glenn Miller wasn't that easily daunted. He was still convinced that somehow he could make it. Stubborn as ever, he tried to prevent the best of his ex-musicians from getting jobs with other leaders, but it was all to no avail. They, like him, had to eat, and if he wasn't paying wages, then someone had to. For Miller himself, money was a real problem. He had sunk his savings, a respectable $18,000, into the band and there was nothing left. If he was to start again, there would certainly have to be outside help. And he was determined to start again. He dropped his old manager, Arthur Michaud, who he had shared with Tommy Dorsey, and signed up with Cy Shribman, a Bostonian who had done wonders for both Artie Shaw and Woody Herman.

With some backing from Shribman and more from Helen's parents who took out a second mortgage on their house, Miller found he had the money needed for another crack at big band success. The pedigree that had seemed so obviously successful twelve months earlier was now merely one more tale of promise unfulfilled. The young musicians he had painfully whipped into shape had gone off in search of safer jobs. He had to discover a new set for the new band. The 'pretty easy climb to the top' had proved an illusion. This time around Miller's band would have to prove itself in the face of far less friendly criticism. But all that maternal sloganeering must have been worth it in the long run. In March 1938, determined to defeat the frustrations of his first-time failure Glenn Miller called up the remaining four members of his first band and set about hiring a new set of musicians and singers. The Glenn Miller Orchestra was on the road again. This time it couldn't fail. It mustn't!

Glen Gray's Casa Loma Orchestra came out of Detroit to pioneer white swing. Yet they ended sweetest of the sweet.

CHAPTER FIVE

BALLROOM BLITZ

IT WAS 1942. The Swing Era's *Annus Mirabilis.* The annual poll held by New York's number one music station, WNEW, read like an honour roll of the nation's musical best and brightest. Harry James, Glenn Miller, Tommy Dorsey, Jimmy Dorsey, Vaughn Monroe, Benny Goodman, Woody Herman, Kay Kyser, Charlie Spivak, Sammy Kaye, Alvino Rey, Claude Thornhill, Gene Krupa, Count Basie, Artie Shaw, Charlie Barnet, Johnny Long, Freddy Martin, Guy Lombardo and Hal MacIntyre. A top twenty leaders who between them represented the whole disparate variety of modes and methods that together made up Swing. Only one star is missing: Duke Ellington. But, as usual, the Duke was strutting on ahead. And just outside the charts came the dozens of second-rank bands, all jostling eagerly for their chance at the big time, their moment of nationwide fame.

The early 1940s saw Swing as entrenched a musical style in America as the 'Liverpool sound' would be in Britain of the early Sixties. There were diversions, there were developments, and other styles of music were already making their play for national favour, but Swing was truly king of the popular music business. Looking at the vast spectrum of the 30's Big Band scene it's possible to list some 450 swing units. Apart from the greats – the Millers, Goodmans, Dorseys, Jameses and so on – there were inumerable outfits who capitalised one way or another on the celebrity or talent of their leader. There were leaders who played piano like Carmen Cavallero and Vincent Lopez; those who played the horn like Muggsy Spanier, Cootie Williams, Louis Armstrong and Ray Anthony. Then there were reed stars, Saxie Dowell, Sam Donahue and Jerry Wald; a few who played violin like Al Donahue and Joe Venuti and others who sang, like Little Jack Little, Skinny Ennis and Orrin Tucker. And naturally, just as the ranks of top soloists produced leaders in their own right, so did the arrangers: Ted Fio Rito, Sy Oliver, Don Redman and several other top creative talents used their sound for their own bands as well as others. And beyond these ex-solo talents who chose to lead their own bands, came the unsung but once loved ranks of even lesser leaders: sidemen who wanted to pick up on the new trend, copycats who capitalised on a national craze and foisted third-rate swing on an ever-hungry public. There were even the despised 'Mickey Mouse' outfits, the least swinging of any bands that era produced; soft-pedalling everything, they played the mid-West 'society' circuits, mocking the whole idea of swing in the music they played, a mere masquerade of the real thing. Still, from the big names to the Mickey Mouse bands, swing could claim that America was its playground. Purists, harking back desperately to 'traditional' (New Orleans) jazz would murmur of 'degenerate Swing' and rebels, working out the new 'bop' sounds at Minton's after hours jam sessions, might deride the formula music of the big bands, but everyone had to accept that Swing was, in its own 'jive talk', hep.

So where did it come from, this national music obsession? After all, ten years earlier, the state of the US music scene looked parlous in the extreme. What had passed as a white version of jazz, epitomised by the misnamed 'King of Jazz' Paul Whiteman (a leader whose real jazz stars, Bix Beiderbecke, Jack Teagarden and others, invariably left him through irritation with his essentially commercial sound) had vanished with the coming of the Depression in 1929. The nation had rushed helter-skelter into an orgy of sentiment and self-pity. Yip Harburg's *Brother, Can You Spare Me A Dime* was the Depression's number one hit. Mawkish in the extreme, but tragically pertinent to the economic horrors of the era, it was a deliberate plunge into the miseries of the time. One British critic pointed out that where 'Brother' was going to get his dime was a moot point, since surely everyone was suffering alike according to the American press, but such jokey scepticism cut no ice across the Atlantic. The Twenties, a glittering Scott Fitzgerald parade, had gone. The dour wasteland of John Steinbeck's Thirties had taken over.

As far as the bands were concerned, the early Thirties were indeed a wasteland. There *was* work for the mass of musicians, epitomised by the career of Glenn Miller, who had started his career when the jazzy Twenties were in full flight; but it was hardly the progressive, exciting work they were looking for. Sessions, gigs for pit orchestras, fill-ins around the various bands which formed, broke up and reformed continually, this was the stuff of the average musician's life around 1932. The powers in the land were the sweet bands. Guy Lombardo and His Royal Canadians, Ozzie Nelson, these were the success stories of the early Thirties. Low key, dependable,

ABOVE: **Prankster Joe Venuti probably topped the all-time jazz violinists' poll. Ex-Jean Goldkette, he did the rounds, including Red Nichols' classic all-star line-ups, and Paul Whiteman's Twenties band. But talent outran discipline and his own band never scored. Venuti then turned to small combos. It made everyone happy.**

ABOVE: **Jimmy and Tommy, the Dorsey Brothers, had talent unlimited but no mutual tolerance. Glenn Miller arranged for them, and they shared a Whiteman apprenticeship with the legendary Bix Beiderbecke (*FACING PAGE*). Unrivalled trumpet virtuoso, Bix died tragically young, destroyed by liquor.**

nothing excessive either on stage or off it. The whole down-tempo style of the Depression years was represented in Lombardo's instruction to his band 'No drinking before midnight'. And in music, as well as in the greater world around it, the time cried out for adventure, experimentation, and above all a mood of optimistic change that would drag America from its mental and economic Depression.

Music is conditioned, like the rest of the entertainment industry, by the situation of the world in which, and for which it is created. When Franklin Delano Roosevelt initiated his New Deal in 1932, the stage was clearly set for the kind of optimistic action that America was looking for. And with that in mind, there was a chance for music to parallel the new feeling in the nation. If self-pity was to be replaced by self-help, then it wasn't surprising that the sweet bands were soon to be knocked off their dubious perch by swing. But before looking at that epochal turn-around in America's musical taste, it's still necessary to look back to the Twenties.

Swing didn't just emerge neat and complete when Benny Goodman, despairing of his regular playlist, turned to the 'hot' arrangements he'd been given by black leader and arranger Fletcher Henderson. That gig at the Palomar Ballroom in Los Angeles on August 21st, 1935 gives one of the few specific dates by which any musical developments can be dated, but really it meant very little. In the first place, the simple fact that Goodman's revolutionary sound came from a black leader whose own band was already a name among those who appreciated 'hot' music by the end of the Twenties showed that what seemed new, was in fact nothing that extra-ordinary by 1935. White kids may not previously have appreciated the sort of music that Goodman brought reluctantly to the stand that August night, but it was all there ready and waiting.

The basic dance-band form of the Twenties set out as a simple statement of a theme, and an unaltered repetition of the same chorus, over and over again. Gradually there developed some improvisation on these

ABOVE: **Jean Goldkette's Band collapsed in 1927. But it nurtured many top swing stars, putting an edge on Twenties white jazz.**

choruses. For all his commercialism, Paul Whiteman deserves some credit for employing special arrangements for standard hits. His example was followed by other leaders; Coon-Sanders, Paul Ash, Abe Lyman among others. They weren't always that good, or particularly original, but they tried. But the really creative bands of the era were black. Duke Ellington, Count Basie, Fletcher Henderson, Bennie Moten and McKinney's Cotton Pickers . . . these were the real progressives of the Twenties. Naturally, since they *were* black, their abilities were confined to the ballrooms and the second-rate halls. The swank hotels didn't want to know. It was their musical loss, though probably their commercial gain. Among whites only the Jean Goldkette and Ben Pollack bands showed any signs of parallel development. Come the Depression, progress of any sort took a hard knock. Sweet music, and its attendant crooners like Rudy Vallee and Bing Crosby held sway. The white musicians who played for Ben Pollack went their various ways, struggling for survival. The black ones, whose creativity may have helped the spirit but didn't do any more towards paying the rent, struggled too. In the early Thirties, that period of intense frustration, the music business languished. But there was one tiny light.

Of all the unlikely spots, white Swing, the gradually expanding movement that started with 'hot' solos in the Twenties, and climaxed with hundreds of big bands twenty years later, found its greatest boost in the Mid West. When Swing really was on top, the mid-West Cities, such as Cleveland and even Chicago, showed themselves unrelentingly puritan in their attitudes to what City Fathers everywhere condemned as 'degenerate' – and for very different reasons from those which jazz purists brought out. But when a breakaway Jean Goldkette outfit, the Detroit-based Orange Blossoms, took off, it was only the knowledgeable fans around the Mid-West who were able to enjoy them. The Orange Blossoms didn't last long under that name. One night they were hired to open at a new club in Canada, the Casa

ABOVE: **Maybe Paul Whiteman wasn't really the 'King of Jazz', but his band promoted the best of the 'hot' musicians.**

Loma, built specially for a visit by the Prince of Wales, who as usual was enjoying himself as much in the New World as he did in the Old. The club didn't open, and the gig wasn't played, but the name must have had some special appeal. Without further ado, the Orange Blossoms, formed into a co-operative under their leader sax-man Glen Gray, became the Casa Loma Orchestra.

The Casa Loma Orchestra, or Glen Gray and the Casa Loma Orchestra as it became after 1934 when the band switched from Okeh to Decca records, proved the most vital link between the 'hot' jazz of the Twenties and the Swing of the mid-Thirties. Obviously the band couldn't survive on an undiluted diet of hot music, and the 'sweet' dominance in the early Thirties wouldn't permit it economically, but with a subtle combination of mellow ballads and progressive 'swing', Casa Loma captured a mass of fans. In 1929 when work ran out in Detroit, they moved to New York and played at Roseland and other big ballrooms. By the advanced standards of the real swing innovators, the black bands, Casa Loma were undeniably corny, but their very flashy, up-tempo music delighted young fans who

ABOVE: **Backed by Glenn Miller, Charlie Spivak's purist trumpet led a popular swing unit. 'Pin-Up Girl' had his boys backing the first lady of pin-up – Betty Grable and her million dollar legs!**

ABOVE: **Nelson Riddle tasted early success when his brilliant arranging talent found its way into the Charlie Spivak outfit.**

found it hard to accept the dreary banalities of the Sweet bands. From 1930-35 the Casa Loma Orchestra enjoyed five years of topflight success and featured on the first ever radio show to appreciate swing music – the Camel Caravan. They also played what was to become the proving ground for all the top swing bands, the Glen Island Casino, and it was Casa Loma who launched the tradition of stage-bands at New York's Paramount Theatre. Yet when Swing was booming, the band had in effect vanished. Perhaps it was played out after an exhausting five years in which swing was still virtually unknown. The annual *Metronome* polls reveal the ironic story of the Casa Loma decline. In 1937 fans ranked them second most popular Swing band and only seventh in the sweet music category. By 1940, when Swing was reaching its peak, Casa Loma had dropped to sixth in the Swing ratings and jumped to second among the sweet bands. It was a sad ending for a band that had once stood almost alone in the face of sweet band supremacy.

Of course Casa Loma wasn't the only white outfit challenging the sweet bands. All those musicians who had been reared by Pol-

ABOVE: **The man with rhythm in his bones, ace drummer Gene Krupa, another Goodman alumnus, went his own way in 1938. Roy Eldridge and Anita O'Day boosted his hot line-up.**

lack, Goldkette or Red Nichols weren't just satisfied to let their talents and ambitions atrophy. As the Depression gave way to the New Deal, the momentum of musical change picked up. The Dorsey Brothers, Jimmy, a Whiteman star, and brother Tommy, once of Jean Goldkette's band, formed their own band, the Dorsey Brothers Orchestra in 1934. With Glenn Miller as their arranger and musical director, their band had much of the Casa Loma sound, but the eternally warring brothers destroyed the band, despite its undoubted potential. In 1935 Tommy Dorsey walked off the stand for the last time. Jimmy stayed with the musicians and Tommy formed his own outfit. In due course, they would both, in their unique ways, provide the Swing era with two of its most exciting bands.

But the responsibility for the real launch of Swing fell to another young star of the 1920s progressive bands. One of twelve children of a Jewish family from Chicago's ghetto district, Benny Goodman was hired by Ben Pollack when he was only 16. And that wasn't even his first professional gig. A member of the Musicians Union from age 13 he had soon established a reputation as a child prodigy as far as his clarinet playing was concerned. Like all his contemporaries in the Swing era, Goodman did the rounds of the best white outfits of the Twenties, then spent the Depression marking time in sessions and pit bands. In 1934 he was scheduled to take an all-star lineup (including Jack Teagarden, Red Norvo, Gene Krupa and Bessie Smith) to Europe, but the tour fell through. In December of that year Goodman's band, culled from the best of the young white musicians and determined to move back to a more genuine type of jazz than the 'sweet' version, won a vital audition. The producer of the Nabisco 'Let's Dance' radio show, a three-hour marathon show, devoted exclusively to dancebands, heard the Goodman Band at their residency at Billy Rose's Music Hall. Along with the Latin sounds of Xavier Cugat and the sweet music of Kel Murray, Goodman's youthful talents made up the third part of the twenty-six week long radio show. Not surprisingly, against the mellow sounds of the other two bands, the Goodman outfit sounded electrifying. It was vital exposure for the band and in May 1935, when the radio gig was over, Goodman's agent decided to get his client a spot in a top hotel. Unfortu-

ABOVE: **Clean-cut Woody Herman, whose musical virtuosity and professional presentation won him the hearts of millions.**

nately the hotel in question was New York's Roosevelt, lately occupied by the sweetest of the sweet, Guy Lombardo. The Goodman Band was given its obligatory two weeks' notice on opening night.

Through late summer 1935 Benny Goodman took his band touring around the country. Cross-country appearances had little impact and by the time Goodman reached the Palomar Ballroom in Los Angeles, he was reaching the end of his tether. Playing the dance-band classics of the time wasn't having any impact; for that kind of music the fans could go elsewhere. Goodman wasn't that good. But at the end of the line, Goodman turned desperately to a side of his band that had hitherto been kept secret. When they had been back in New York the band had cut some classic sides that were pure Swing. Arranged by Fletcher Henderson, whose style was to dominate so many of the white bands, Benny Goodman's Band recorded, among other great sides, 'Blue Skies', 'Sometimes I'm Happy' and 'King Porter Stomp'. When the Palomar crowd remained bored by his regulation numbers, Goodman let rip with 'King Porter Stomp'. It was the birth of a new era. The kids went wild and Benny Goodman could do no wrong. By the end of 1935 Swing was on the way, and Goodman was already progressing towards his popular title, 'The King of Swing'.

The progress of the Goodman Band was as meteoric as was the rise of Swing and is too complex to be charted in detail. The kind of overnight rags-to-riches escalation in the fortune of the new bands can be seen elsewhere—in the fortunes of Glenn Miller's Orchestra in 1939. Hotel gigs followed one another, Goodman's records filled the shops with eager buyers, his concerts sold out within hours. By the *Metronome* Poll of 1936, Goodman was outvoting Casa Loma by two votes to one. Featuring solo stars like trumpeter Harry James and drummer Gene Krupa, the Goodman Band delighted audiences from coast to coast. And when Goodman formed his Benny Goodman Quartet, a hot band within a hot band, to feature two black stars—Lionel Hampton (vibes), Teddy Wilson (piano)—as well as Krupa and himself, Goodman showed that he certainly hadn't forgotten just who really set the Swing era in motion.

Perhaps the supreme moment of many great Goodman appearances of this era was the world-famous Carnegie Hall concert of January 16th, 1938. Replacing for the night John Barbirolli's Philharmonic Orchestra in the classical music's holy of holies set the seal on Goodman's stardom. The concert started slowly, but soon built into a grooving, swinging outpouring of the new music. From the stalls to the gods, the audiences were shagging (as Swing's own dance was called) while they sat in their seats. In the boxes, distinguished Carnegie Hall patrons were swept away in the glorious sound and joined in the dancing, cheering, applauding, ecstatic mob.

Ironically, the success of the Carnegie Hall concert set off a couple of internally troubled years for the band. Gene Krupa quit to form his own band and play the music the way he wanted it. Personnel changes became the order of the day, and in 1940 what might be called the 'Original' Benny Goodman Band was broken up. In 1941 he came back, with a new lineup and a new sound, but as the poll of 1942 has shown, Glenn Miller and Harry James, among others, had captured the top spots.

With its blend of 'hot' and dance music, though with the emphasis mainly on the 'hot', the Goodman band was a quintessential Swing outfit. It came with the right sound at the right moment in time. It was helped by the nationwide exposure that a top radio spot could bring, and with that one instance of

ABOVE: **Eccentric showman Guy Lombardo in his personalised speedboat.** *FACING PAGE:* **Cab Calloway—'Prince of Heigh-de-ho'.**

luck, the Palomar Ballroom, without which even the greatest talents may founder forever, it brought Swing to a mass audience. Benny Goodman himself was also typical of the top big band leaders. He was an astute businessman, a demanding musician, and a tough disciplinarian. Without these three qualities, no Swing band could really hope to hit the top and stay there. Such a combination of skills, none of which include spontaneous musical genius, undoubtedly helps those critics of Swing who claim that it was too formalised. Yet Swing bands did change; they had to, considering the continual turnover of personnel, and Goodman's was no exception. Whereas the band that on the one hand was the most musically original and progressive, Duke Ellington's Orchestra was, on the other, the one whose stars and sidemen remained most stable throughout the era.

In Goodman's wake came literally hundreds of Swing bands. There were the first generation leaders, the white musicians who had been soloists and sidemen for Pollack, Whiteman, Goldkette or Nichols. Then came a second generation, the sidemen of these leaders—Harry James and Gene Krupa, both of whom starred with Goodman; Ray Eberle who had once sang with Miller; Tony Pastor who learnt with Artie Shaw and many, many others. They ranged from the 'pure' Swing of Goodman, a development from Twenties danceband music, only replacing the old emphasis on ballads with a new one of 'hot' playing. Or, like Woody Herman they based their style around the blues, a blues much sweetened and smoothed down by the big band treatment. Or Bob Crosby, who took over much of Pollack's old band and took for his new style a Dixieland influenced sound. And Charlie Barnet who openly copied Ellington and Basie. And there were still the sweet bands, like Kay Kyser who aped Lombardo, and enjoyed similar popularity. Swing is so widespread a term it's easy to forget how vast a musical umbrella it spreads over so much diversity.

Why did Swing triumph so emphatically? In a phrase, the time was ripe. The musicians were there, and had been for a decade. The musical style was waiting there in the wings with them. But until the mid-Thirties there simply wasn't the right social atmosphere for the free and easy, exciting Swing sound to catch on. Depression, in the head or in the pocket, doesn't go well with up-tempo jollity. Swing, at its best, was not meant to be soothing. The lifeless, depressing music of the early Thirties, enlivened only by breakaway bands like the Casa Loma Orchestra, couldn't possibly go on indefinitely, just as the Depression which spawned it had to end some time. When it did start to ease up and FDR's New Deal brought the country back to life, there was this ready-made, optimistic, good-time, get-up-and-dance sound just waiting for life to improve.

While there was a vast number of Swing bands, and a wide diversity of styles, as far as actually producing 'swinging' music was concerned, the best of the black bands of the late Twenties and early Thirties had probably reached the peaks in that direction. Ellington, Basie, Bennie Moten whose recordings of 1932 are often cited as supreme 'swinging' music, set a style which the white bands never really bettered on a creative level. Where the white Swing bands had the edge was in all the benefits that stemmed simply from their being white. They could afford better equipment, they could play a far wider variety of venues, they were given priority treatment wherever they went, they had the radio almost as their sole province. What happened with the white Swing explosion was that a particular adaptation of 'Hot' playing by big black bands was taken to a level of technical virtuosity that had never been seen before and, since the decline of most big bands, will never be repeated in the same way. The growth of radio, of increasingly sophisticated recording techniques and better record production meant that the public was more able to pick and choose the artists they would enjoy. New standards were set and the top Swing bands fought to reach and surpass them.

Where top Swing bands did gain their independent sounds was in their use of three vital ingredients. Sidemen, who graduated in this period first becoming starring soloists and then perhaps leaders in their own right; vocalists, the crooners and canaries who are dealt with elsewhere, and above all arrangers. With-

Coleman Hawkins set the style for swinger Charlie Barnet (*ABOVE*) who was later to lead the "Blackest White Band of All".

out an arranger a leader and his musicians and vocalists were in limbo. Goodman's Los Angeles breakthrough came when he used the snappy, swinging arrangements he had picked up from that master of the craft, Fletcher Henderson. Glenn Miller, whose instrumental talents were perhaps not quite of the very greatest, was an arranger of genius. All of the top leaders, unless they were arrangers themselves, such as Duke Ellington whose portmanteau talents embraced every side of the big band experience, needed this most vital of right-hand men.

And arrangers, with their different styles, gave bands their different characters. Fletcher Henderson depended on a call and response style. Don Redman and Eddie Sauter, like Ellington, were more involved with a new style of voicings for the instruments, taking them out of their usual sections and blending the various sounds for an overall new appeal. Glenn Miller's use of an extra clarinet and sax instead of trumpets has been immortalised as 'The Miller Sound', and when commercial pressures took over, arrangers Bill Finegan and Billy May kept up the good work. Some of today's top names in the music business learnt their trade in the Swing era: Nelson Riddle with Charlie Spivak, Henry Mancini for Tex Beneke, Ray Conniff and Johnny Mandel for Artie Shaw. All of them, in their special ways, gave bands that extra flavour that turned competent musicians into chart-topping headliners. Swing, despite the occasional European venture, was essentially an American phenomenon. What tastes of Swing Europe did enjoy came almost solely from touring American bands. To start a craze for good-time music you first need a bad time to make the improvement necessary. Europe had felt the Depression but never to so savage an extent as had America. And after the bad, a period of optimism is needed. In Europe by 1935 the likelihood of another war was almost a foregone conclusion, however much governmental propaganda might try to blur the facts. In America the New Deal, not to mention three thousand miles of water, put such gloomy thoughts to the backs of the minds of all but a few pessimists. And they weren't the sort to be listening to Swing anyway. For the public Swing was the tonic they needed, along with Amos 'n' Andy, the Funny Pages and Hollywood. For the musicians it was a necessary tonic too. Twenties jazz had been a saccharine affair amongst most white bands. Now Thirties' Swing gave so many frustrated 'hot' musicians the chance to show what they were made of. As the breadth and intensity of the Swing explosion proved beyond a doubt, there was no-one, from the greatest to the least, who wasn't desperate to do just that.

CHAPTER SIX

SUCCESS

THERE'S THIS SCENE in 'The Glenn Miller Story': The new Miller band, 1938 vintage, are sitting through some endless rehearsal. The crummy basement is stacked with chairs and tables pushed to one side as the musicians try yet again to get 'the sound' that Glenn Miller/ Jimmy Stewart is urging. Suddenly, a yell! A trumpeter, is it Bob Price? bangs his instrument on a music stand. It rebounds into his face and cuts his lip. There's no way he can play. Quick as a flash Glenn throws in a new arrangement, 'let's put the reeds over the brass!' They try it. . . it works. A snappy all-night arranging session in his hotel room and come the gig next day, there it is! The Glenn Miller sound, neat and complete. And from thereon in, of course, it's one long bed of roses, royalty cheques and record-breaking attendances.

It's also totally fictional. When Miller put together his new band in the Spring of 1938 he was as determined as ever to succeed. And success, he knew all too well, came from giving the kids something they hadn't heard before. Goodman had already had the limelight for almost three years. Other classy swing outfits had joined him up there amongst the money and the adulation. Miller's first efforts to join the big timers had failed. In the end the band had nothing to offer. This time around, things were going to be different. There would be no 'prima donnas', no smart-ass individualists who would go their own sweet, boozy ways and wreck the perfection for which their leader was inevitably striving. Miller wanted young, malleable talents whom he could make into one band he wanted and whom once the band was created, he could control.

He kept only four of his old lineup. Rolly Bundock on bass, Bob Price as first trumpet, Chummy Macgregor, that perennial buddy in the movie, on piano and Hal MacIntrye on first saxophone. That was it for the veterans. Then he started picking up his new boys. And in many cases they really weren't much more than boys. When war, and with it the draft turned up three years later, the Miller band's young personnel were gutted by Uncle Sam's demands. Only Macgregor and the leader were actually ineligible as far as age was concerned.

Among the youngsters he drafted into his lineup were Willie Schwartz whose preferred instrument was the sax but who was mainly used on clarinet. Then there was Gordon 'Tex' Beneke, one of Miller's all-time favourites, to join the sax section. And a young singer, Ray Eberle, brother of Jimmy Dorsey's crooner, Bob Eberly. The full story of Eberle's unhappy relationship with Miller has been told elsewhere, as has that of his 'canary', Marion Hutton, but his hiring of the relatively mediocre young singer shows one of those strange lapses of judgement to which Miller continually proved himself a victim. He hired Ray Eberle because be needed a singer, fair enough, and because he was Bob Eberly's brother which therefore, by Glenn's logic, should have made him equally talented. As it turned out the Miller instant judgment, which could prejudice him for years either for or against a musician (or anyone else) on just a brief meeting, proved a great mistake. Eberle never hit the heights that his leaders demanded and in the end, their parting was a stormy one.

That, and other dramas, both good and bad, still lay in the future. As Miller rehearsed his new boys back at the Haven Studios where his first outfit had put their act together, he kept looking for the right sound. In all fairness, he never set out to be a redhot swinging combo. He knew, as a good Middle American naturally realised, that there was nothing quite like the middle way for wooing the fans.

While 'The Glenn Miller Story' is a dubious source of the actual facts, it's true, of course, that there was a 'Miller Sound'. The point was that it didn't simply appear, *deus ex machina,* one lucky day in 1938. The scoring for reeds over brass had been an old Miller arranging technique since his days with Ray Noble. The facts, as ever with such massively reiterated myths, are simple. Noble had a trumpeter, one Peewee Erwin, who had a mania for playing the high notes. To accommodate him Miller scored his parts an octave higher than normal. When Erwin left the band, his replacement couldn't handle the high pieces. To compensate Miller used two clarinets instead, backed up by an extra tenor sax. When his first band went out with Irving Fazola on clarinet, Miller used this type of arranging to give the talented musician more chances to show off his skills. And when the second band were working up their performance, Miller decided that this reversal of the

Miller's band at last hit the top, but somehow the leader never picked the number one artistes. Singer Ray Eberle (*BELOW*) couldn't rival his talented brother Bob, though Miller willed him to win. In the end the bitter parting was always inevitable.

AS
NF

usual roles of brass and reed sections would be the anchor for their sound. This would serve ideally as the unique aspect of the new Miller band that would hopefully take it from obscurity to fame.

Hopefully, indeed. The new Glenn Miller Orchestra opened in Boston at the dingy Raymor Ballroom, right back where the first outfit had foundered a year before. Chick Webb was playing Levaggi's and Artie Shaw was starring at the Roseland-State ballroom. It wasn't an auspicious start. In June they moved up a fraction, geographically anyway. The Paradise Restaurant, on Broadway just above 49th Street, was a New York venue, but that was about all you could say for it. Definitely off the seamy end of the booking list, it starred a down-at-heel bunch of chorines and catered mainly for out-of-town tourists and businessmen. To add insult to injury, Miller's band was second on the bill. Stars of the show were Freddie Fisher and His Schnickelfritzers, an outfit strictly for the sticks.

For the rest of the summer of 1938 the Miller youngsters struggled against a number of second-rate gigs. Reed's Casino in Asbury Park, where kids hurled cotton snowballs at the stage, Hamid's Million Dollar Pier, where the whole week grossed only twelve hundred dollars. That was the style of the new band. The unique sound didn't seem to be cutting any ice and the bitching was starting even sooner than the last time around.

In September it did seem as if the tide of miseries was consenting to recede just marginally. Cy Shribman, who had already lent Miller some money to start the new band, agreed to become a permanent financier. Shribman, who ran a whole chain of ballrooms with his brother Joe, was one of those larger than life characters who seem hand-reared by the business side of the entertainment world. He went from hall to hall, picking up the receipts for the night, stuffing the wads in his pocket, paying off the bands as he went, and never making any mistakes in his very personal accounting system. Nor did he make many errors in his judgement of bands. He had already helped the careers of such top liners as Artie Shaw, Woody Herman and Tommy Dorsey. Now he agreed to pick up the $12,000 Miller already owed on the new band and look after their future backing in return for a quarter of Miller's profits. It seems a large chunk of the orchestra, but it meant steady money, and with Shribman's chain of big band venues, even more important—steady work. On top of this, came another boost: Miller signed his band to RCA Victor for their future recordings. Nothing had gone right with their previous company, Brunswick, but RCA, spear-headed by its astute recording director Eli Oberstein had a reputation of doing well with swing bands.

That same month the Miller band moved into a regular two-day a week spot at Boston's Roseland—State Ballroom, owned by the Shribman brothers. They weren't exactly a major draw—only 300 a night turned up, peanuts compared with glories in store—but the Roseland provided the regular radio exposure that any band needed. Pay was still minimal, some fifty dollars a week a head, but in December 1938 the band finished in the black. It was the first time either of Miller's personal ventures had actually come out ahead. If nothing else it seemed like a comforting sign.

But on the whole 1938 had been a depressing year, and 1939 didn't start off to well either. Desperate for a New York showplace, and knowing that any radio show was good for the band, Miller put his men back in the seedy Paradise Restaurant and at a fee of some seventy-five dollars *less* than the previous booking. One good thing did happen at this time, though no-one realised it when it happened. Tom Sheils, a pushy young booker for his school, Iona Prep in New Rochelle, booked the Miller band for a one-night gig. The kids in general and Tom Sheils in particular loved the band. Fired up with enthusiasm, Sheils, who happened to be the son of a Supreme Court Judge for Westchester County, rushed off to Michael DeZutter, owner of the Glen Island Casino and begged him to book Miller for the next summer season. Shiels reasoned that the Miller band were on the way to becoming a cult success with the perceptive swing fans who flocked to DeZut-

FACING PAGE: Artie Shaw loved the bands and hated the business. It didn't make for an easy life.

ter's ballroom every summer. Why not hire them and keep everyone happy. DeZutter said he would think about it.

The most encouraging event in early 1939 was undoubtedly the results of the latest *Metronome* magazine poll of top musicians. The band was not featured, but Miller himself earned the number four overall trombone rating. As far as jazz trombones were concerned he was rated second. His superior, inevitably, was Jack Teagarden.

Miller remained dissatisfied with the band. They were too loose and the horrors of the Paradise shows hadn't helped their self-respect any. He wanted perfection and they were hoping for a hike in their wages. Neither side seemed to be getting what they were after. But Shribman found them another job, this time at Frank Dailey's Meadbrook Ballroom in New Jersey. And gradually, very gradually, they *were* catching on. The Iona Prep dance had been just one small step in the right direction. Now Martin Block, the influential disc jockey who ran WNEW's 'Make Believe Ballroom', a swing showcase second to none, was starting to play Miller records. The band had picked up a new arranger, Bill Finegan, and his inspired versions of popular favourites helped the band in its way. Though Miller, competitive as ever, was never really happy with his talented arranger. Unlike Finegan, who preferred spontaneous composition and arrangement, Miller was a stickler for the rigid forms of the Schillinger system, in which all arrangements were based on a mathematical method. Miller, always working strictly to his own book of rules, was unable to understand Finegan's method and countered by editing everything he did. It hardly promoted a happy partnership.

On March 1st, 1939, co-incidentally Glenn Miller's thirty-fifth birthday, came the turning point for Miller's band. Manager Mike Nidorf, who had come from the Rockwell-O'Keefe Agency, later renamed GAC, rang to tell Miller that Tom Shiels' recommendation had paid off. Starting May 1939, the Glenn Miller Orchestra would be playing a season at the Glen Island Casino. It was just what the band needed. The best, most knowledgable audience, and the most extensive radio net-

Woody Herman (*ABOVE*) played professional sax since he was nine years old. Via vaudeville and Isham Jones, Herman set up

working available.

But first there was the Meadowbrook residency. While the Glen Island Casino has been spotlighted as the start of the Miller success story, and certainly it was, the bandwagon was starting to move even earlier. Meadowbrook too had a large and discerning young audience and they liked what they heard from the Miller boys. Owner Frank Dailey extended the stay from four to seven weeks and as the band played steadily together in the same place there's no doubt that they became a stronger and more cohesive unit. It was perfect preparation for the Glen Island gig. To add to their potential success, April saw the recording of some of Miller's first great single hits. Finegan's version of "Little Brown Jug', the band's popular 'Pavanne,' and a track called 'Now I Lay Me Down to Weep', which had been retitled 'Moonlight Serenade' for the record.

On May 17th the Glenn Miller Orchestra opened at the Glen Island Casino. They closed fourteen weeks later on August 23rd. And the up and coming band who arrived left

his own outfit. Above all, Herman's flexible leadership gave all his talented musicians a chance to show what they could do.

as the most successful unit the ballroom had ever hosted. Miller had reached the kind of technical perfection, if not emotional spontaneity, that he had been looking for by the time the band arrived at the Casino. The weeks at Meadowbrook had ironed out most of the problems, and with Miller's instinctive knowledge of a good commercial set, including the first of his classic 'Something Old, Something New, Something Borrowed, Something Blue' complications, he had the kids eating out of his hand. The radio show made sure that the rest of the country heard the good news and very soon it was apparent to the band and its backers that at long last the Glenn Miller story had really begun to look good.

It's impossible to say exactly why a band, any band, takes off. Glen Island did for Miller what Los Angeles' Palomar Ballroom had done for Benny Goodman four years earlier. When the band left Glen Island Casino they were established with the greatest. The 1,200 fans who crammed the ballroom for the last show gave Miller and his band a party to celebrate the season and to thank them for a summer's glorious music. It was an unprecedented event in the Casino's history. In that summer's WNEW poll, the band found themselves the fourth most popular among New York area listeners. They fell behind Goodman, Shaw and Tommy Dorsey, but had jumped in in front of Jimmy Dorsey, Harry James, Count Basie, Sammy Kaye, Gene Krupa and the rest. The *Metronome* poll showed them fifth in the swing section and fourth in the sweet. In the Favourite of All voting they came out fifth. It was a creditable performance for a band who had scraped in the year before with positions in those same categories of eighteenth, twenty-sixth and thirty-seventh respectively!

There had only been one thing wrong with the Glen Island gig—the money was minimal. But with the kind of reputation that the fourteen weeks on Long Island had given them, money problems would soon be irrelevant. After Glen Island they went straight into Loew's Capitol Theatre in Washington, DC. The first week's gross totalled out at a massive $22,500. Next at the Hippodrome Theatre in Baltimore for the first week of September the band attracted an audience of 19,000 to their shows. After Baltimore came a record-breaking series of one-night stands. In Syracuse, NY; Hershey, Pennsylvania; Bristol, Connecticut—everywhere the band went they smashed through previous box office and attendance records. The climax of this early burst came at the top-ranking venue of them all—New York City's Paramount Theatre in Times Square. Sharing the bill with the Inkspots, the Glenn Miller band notched up a three week gross of $150,000!! They were immediately booked for a return in 1940, and a substantial guarantee of $6,500 per week.

The history of the Glenn Miller Orchestra at this juncture tends to look something like a bunch of telephone numbers. They could do no wrong. The fans poured into every venue they played; they were coining money. One music paper called Miller 'the Cinderella Man' of the music business. One thing was sure. When the band had gone into the Glen Island Casino, just three months before the world started lying prostrate at their feet, Cinderella had just walked slap bang into

Jimmie Lunceford's swinging band blew the greatest contenders off stage when it came to the battles of the big-time bands. But black bands never achieved the exposure and the rewards of their white rivals. Lunceford died as he lived on the road.

CHAPTER SEVEN

UPTOWN SAT'DAY NIGHT

GLENN MILLER, Benny Goodman, the Dorseys, Artie Shaw . . . as the top white leaders took their big bands around the country spreading the gospel of Swing to an enthusiastic America, there must have been a few wry grins across the faces of their black counterparts. For, in the very same manner that the white rock musicians of the 1960s were so often echoes of their black predecessors of the previous decade, so were the big Swing bands of the late Thirties enormously indebted to styles set by black orchestras of the Twenties and early Thirties.

Jazz had developed from black roots and a whole generation of musicians who were to lead and play in the great Swing bands, both black and white, had gained their first love of this type of music through listening to the early black jazzmen. But originality meant little in the face of a social system which dumped the black man, whatever his abilities, right on the bottom of the ladder. The average black was simply looked down upon; the talented ones were tolerated, praised to some extent, but never really given their dues, let alone their equality. Stock figures like the movie actor Stepin Fetchit set the tone for the pre-war image of 'the Negro'.

Naturally, the low status the black population had been given didn't mean that they weren't of some use to white America. And not simply as servants. Few New Yorkers venture north of Manhattan's 90th Street these days, but in the Twenties and Thirties there was nowhere quite like Harlem, liberal photographer Carl van Vechten's 'Nigger Heaven', if you were white, rich, and looking for a good time with just a touch of adventure thrown in.

As far as the young white sophisticates were concerned, Harlem, which in those days was centred on 133rd Street rather than on today's all-black mecca at 125th, was tailor-made for having yourself a really good time. With its speakeasies, nightclubs, brothels and jazz joints, it had all the ingredients of high-tone slumming. Of course the average white trendsetter didn't get to see the 'real' Harlem. They saw what he or she wanted to see: low-life blacks putting on a gaudy, bawdy show fulfilling, for a price, every fancy stereotype that white liberal trendsetters could desire. The rat-infested tenement blocks that made up most of the ghetto were *their* problem. It was easier to blind yourself in the gaudy neon of the main streets.

It didn't matter much where you went. Smalls Paradise, the Savoy Ballroom, Dicky Wells', the Heatwave, Jerry's Log Cabin . . . the joints were much the same. There the rich whites would meet Harlem's 'sporting crowd', a mishmash of underworld characters—pimps, hustlers and whores—and probably a good proportion of the downtown 'smart set', straight out of the junior age-group of the Social Register. Not all of the 'sporting crowd' were merely there to rip off whitey, though ambitious blacks had little alternative if they didn't want to end up as Pullman porters or servants in the rich white households. As Bumpy Johnson, Harlem's number one 'sportsman' of the Thirties put it: 'We ain't in no zoo. How would you like it if we was to go downtown to your clubs and restaurants to stare at you people?' But for the most part, being stared at was the price Harlemites had to accept as the due they paid for plucking the pockets of their white patrons. There were a few all-black clubs, the Savoy Ballroom, Leroy's and the Alhambra Bar and Grill, but they were few and far between. More typical might be Clinton Moore's. This particular hangout to which titled English males flocked 'like homing pigeons' as Helen Lawrenson has put it in an *Esquire* piece, featured a pianist named Joey. Apart from singing and playing Joey really thrilled his white clientele with his speciality act. Lowering his trousers he would sit slowly down on a candle until it disappeared neatly between his buttocks. To have seen Joey's vanishing trick must have 'made' innumerable dinner parties back in London.

But of all the clubs and speakeasies which dragged the thrill-seekers uptown to Harlem, none had so distinguished a reputation as the Cotton Club. Planned as a ballroom and once run as the 'Club de Luxe' by ex-World Heavyweight Champion Jack Johnson, the Club, situated on the corner of 142nd Street and Lennox Avenue, had a reputation throughout the swinging Western hemisphere. With its high salaries, its glamorous showgirls and top name acts, the Cotton Club attracted the cream of contemporary white society from resident America and visiting Europe. It didn't on the other hand, have many blacks except for those on the bandstand, the floorshow, and serving the food and drinks. The Cotton Club, epitome of the Harlem playland, was strictly for whites only.

In all fairness, not all the visitors to Harlem came straight off the tourist buses that ran

Everyone knew Louis Armstrong (*ABOVE*). Ironically the ace trumpeter never fronted a top-line band. While the Big Bands topped the polls, Satchmo fronted all-star groups, blew his horn or sang duets with other top liners. In every way, he stood alone.

FACING PAGE: There were no comparisons with Edward Kennedy 'Duke' Ellington. From his youth with the 'Washingtonians' through to his worldwide fame that spanned a forty-year career at the top, the Duke was out there by himself. Working around top soloists like Cootie Williams (*ABOVE*) with his 'growl trumpet' and Johnny Hodges, on alto sax, the Ellington style surpassed everyone else, black or white, in the Swing scene. Multi-talented Ellington tailored his creativity to the demands and abilities of his talented lineup. Freedom of expression was what mattered. The Duke of Jazz hobnobbed with Kings, Queens and national leaders. Miller and Goodman might top the polls, but Ellington's band put them to shame. It don't mean a thing, declared the Duke, if it ain't got that swing. He knew exactly what he was talking about.

up through Manhattan in the same way as the rubber-necking visitors would come on their guided tours of San Francisco's Haight-Ashbury thirty-odd years later. Carl van Vechten, for all the apparent racism of his novel's title—'Nigger Heaven'—was in fact the perfect well-meaning liberal. His personal taste in lithe black boys may have endeared him to Harlem for more self-gratifying reasons, but he was undoubtedly one of those whites who *did* catch a glimpse of ghetto life and who genuinely wanted to improve it. With the other whites, he backed the 'Urban League' to help better the lot of black slum dwellers. Well-meaning to the point of embarrassment, it was never more than a spit in the ocean of ghetto miseries. Van Vechten's series of portraits of Bessie Smith have proved a more enduring memorial.

A taste for the artificial glamour of Harlem night-life did not, however, guarantee a massive success for the black bands that the sophisticates and the tourists trooped up to hear. The very fact that one could, all too often, only see and hear these bands in 'whites only' black clubs in New York's Harlem ghetto made this point clear enough. It was all well and good making one's way up to Connie's Inn, Small's or the Cotton Club to check out the fashionable black dance music. It was something else again to relax overnight a rigid social system that was racist by implication even in those parts of the country where, unlike the South, it was not actually racist as an article of faith. By rights the Swing era which can be said to have arrived with Benny Goodman's breakthrough in 1935 should have been well underway a decade before. That is was not was the result not of slovenly musical development, but the cultural as well as social implications of America's policy towards its blacks.

To give Goodman and the other top Swing bandleaders their due, they were never slow to give credit to those blacks who had pioneered a sound and styles that needed the patronage of, white, musicians before developing into a national musical obsession. That Goodman himself employed the unique arranging talents of the enigmatic Fletcher Henderson makes this point with sufficient clarity. Henderson's easy style, with plenty of brass and saxes working in counterpoint to produce the overall swinging effect set a fashion for all the white Swing bands of the era. Ironically by the time his contribution to Swing was really making itself felt, Henderson's own days as a top bandleader were pretty much over. In the Twenties he had fronted a band that boasted such great black artists as Louis Armstrong, Coleman Hawkins, Cootie Williams and included a banjoist called Clarence Holiday—Billie Holiday's father. Yet something was missing despite all that talent and plenty more. Perhaps it was the hard-edged discipline and business ability that typified the truly successful Swing bands, both black and white. Certainly Henderson had no place in his band for the degree of control Ellington or Jimmie Lunceford exercised. And, of course, there was the very simple fact of his being black. No-one could deny that talented or not, there was never any doubt that Henderson's arrangements stood a far greater chance of success when channelled through Benny Goodman than when performed by his own musicians of the Thirties.

Fletcher Henderson may have been the unsung influence behind the white bands of the Thirties, but Edward Kennedy 'Duke' Ellington both rivalled and surpassed them. The popular black stereotype of the time may have been a subservient downtrodden cypher, but the Duke had no time for that. Flamboyant in dress and in his speech, he never grinned or shuffled to amuse the white folks. The foundation of his undying fame may have been laid at the Harlem excursioneer's Cotton Club but that didn't mean that Duke ever did anything but exactly what *he* wanted. Of all the Swing bands, whether black or white, early or late in the era, the Duke Ellington Orchestra tops the bill every time. White bands may have been more popular around the country but the connoisseurs knew what the real thing was. 'It don't mean a thing if it ain't got that Swing' declaimed Ellington back in 1932, and no-one had 'that Swing' like he did.

Edward Kennedy Ellington was born on April 29th, 1899, the son of a government blueprint expert, in Washington, D.C. He learnt piano from a lady called Mrs. Klings-

L-R, ABOVE: Cozy Cole (drums), Jack Teagarden (trombone), Satchmo (trumpet), Artell Shaw (string bass), Barney Bigard (clarinet), Earl Hines (piano). Black and white lineups were still the exception and not the rule. But all-star combos like this one, or Louis Armstrong's longtime teaming with Miller nemesis Jack Teagarden (TOP) gave eager fans a taste of the best of both worlds. But colourwise the Big Bands swung one way or the other. Socially, economically, and of course musically, it was a whole different bag.

dale and soon showed a precocious ability in improvising his own off-beat style. In high school he composed the 'Soda Fountain Rag', which was conceived spontaneously while playing as a pick-up pianist at Washington's Poodle Dog Cafe. Offered a scholarship to art school, he promptly rejected it and took the decision that determined the rest of his life. Nicknamed 'Duke' in his teens as a testimony to his love of sharp clothes, Ellington formed a band called 'Duke's Serenaders'. It was the beginning of a career in music that lasted right up to his death in 1974.

ABOVE: Young Basie's looseness and spontaneity were, by white standards, way out of line. Swing meant discipline, not decadence.

ABOVE: Count Basie had his lean times but still managed to come out ahead, hosting such talents as Sarah Vaughan.

In 1924 he quit musically conservative Washington for the big city challenge of New York and joined up with a band paradoxically called The Washingtonians, a 'hot' quintet who specialised in the 'jungle style' that epitomised good Twenties jazz. He played around the town's small clubs, often in someone's apartment as background for a rent party or similar get-together. And he kept on learning his art, using two private teachers, 'Doc' Perry, a black violinist, and Will Cooke. As the Washingtonians played their regular gig at the Kentucky Club, Ellington and his band began to develop their reputation. But it was December 4th, 1927 that marks the real start of the Duke's glory. King Oliver, greatest black jazzband leader of the early Twenties was offered a residency at the prestigious Cotton Club. He turned it down as a cheap gig. The fledgling Ellington Band had no such reservations. It was a momentous decision for both men. Oliver's fortunes kept on fading away, but for Duke Ellington, his years at the Cotton Club, from December 1927 to February 1931, proved the making of Swing's number one star attraction.

For the young band, the Cotton Club was the perfect environment in which to build up their reputation and their repertoire. Financial stability helped for a start, but the exposure was even more useful. Ellington began to develop and broaden his massive talent and in the years they were at the Club, the band made some 150 records in 64 sessions—a visit to the studios every two and a half weeks. With

Ellington's signature tune 'East St. Louis Toodle-oo', there was 'Jungle Jamboree', 'Harlemania' and 'Big House Blues'. Later came the Ellington masterpieces, 'Mood Indigo' and 'Solitude'.

Once established at the Cotton Club, Ellington never needed to look back. Undoubtedly the sophisticated white audiences helped his progress enormously. He had the talent, although so did Fletcher Henderson; but the exposure to 'society' gave him an acclaim that other black musicians couldn't hope for. When he quit the Cotton Club and toured England and France the success story continued unchecked. If anything, European audiences raved even more than their American cousins. But then to Europe the blacks, American ones anyway, were an exotic and delightful species, not a race to be despised and denigrated.

With such stars as trumpeter Bubber Miley, on whose 'growl' style much of the early Cotton Club hits were based, and Johnny Hodges (sax) and Barney Bigard (clarinet) Ellington's unique music. Under his direction it became a tight unit whose musicians were very much welded into the whole concept of the Ellington style. Top white soloists might move easily from band to band and still find conditions much the same. Once you joined Ellington, you entered a world apart. The leader himself was a musical polymath. Outstanding as pianist, arranger and composer, he also commanded a tough business attitude which made sure that his band always obtained its dues. To many jazz fans Ellington was a true genius. And as a genius he provided music that was not only creatively a step beyond anything his contemporaries could manage, but equally so it was just that bit outside the mainstream style as well. He knew—unlike most other leaders—how valuable were his soloists, and he capitalised on their talents, letting the band as a whole and the musicians as individuals develop to the greatest possible extent. Proficiency in sight-reading or musical technicalities didn't matter that much; what was really important was making the very best of his own and his artists'

Saxman Lester Young (*ABOVE*) starred in Count Basie's collection of talents. As a bonus, he took good care of songbird Billie Holiday.

Johnny Hodges (*ABOVE*) played alto sax for Duke Ellington from 1928 through till the end. A pillar of Ellington's greatness.

true talents. The unit was forged and its music still triumphs over every contemporary. Moving beyond the conservative format of most Swing bands intro/solo/finale Ellington created finely textured sound with his soloists free to improvise within a subtle ensemble background. There were few jazz standards in an Ellington performance, only his own.

Yet despite all this musical expertise, business acumen and talented bandleading, Ellington still had to face one simple fact: like Henderson, like Count Basie, like Jimmie Lunceford, Ellington and his band were black. And as such they were shut off from the rewards that Miller, Goodman, the Dorseys and other top white leaders were reaping throughout the Swing era. Bands like those of Basie and Lunceford might well outplay most of their white rivals, but the public never knew it. If anything the great public thought they weren't even as good as the white bands. And that isn't surprising. With poor wages, since black bands were always paid less than white ones, and fewer gigs to play, the black leaders couldn't afford to buy the quality of instruments that white units could obtain. Their sound suffered accordingly, and so did their reputations.

Even so, with the benefit of hindsight, it's easy to see now that Ellington, Basie and Lunceford, the three leading black bands of the Thirties, really did put their white rivals in the shade as far as excitement and creativity were concerned. The Count Basie Band of 1937-40 must rank with Ellington as one of the most exciting outfits a Swing fan could hear at that time. Bill Basie was first known in 1929 as a major influence on the Bennie Moten Band which he had joined at the same time as its arranger, Eddie Durham. When Moten's band faded away in 1934, 'Count' Basie (a title taken in the tradition of many black leaders of the time) took over. Backed by Columbia's John Hammond who had heard them on radio, the Basie band made their debut at the Grand Terrace in Chicago. Then they moved to New York to play at the Roseland Ballroom. Real stardom came when the band moved into the Savoy Ballroom, reinforced with new personnel in 1937.

Basie's stars, Dicky Wells (trombone),

Later his club was the hippest hangout in Harlem, but first Dickie Wells (*ABOVE*) played topline trombone for Basie and Benny Carter.

Buck Clayton (*ABOVE*, with Babs Gonzales) played trumpet with the Count Basie band. He was just one of the Count's all-stars. Bennie Moten's (*FACING BOTTOM*) Kansas City band launched several black greats. Among others was Count Basie (*FACING TOP*). Basie's freewheeling collection of talents modelled themselves on the pioneering Moten style. Rhythmic and melodic, the Count's bands have always been out there swinging.

Buck Clayton (trumpet) and Lester Young (sax), as well as singer Jimmy Rushing who was joined for a while by Billie Holiday, played music heavily influenced by the Moten Band and by the Moten's South-Western origins. Thus the Basie sound, accentuated by Moten's old arranger Eddie Durham, was full of blues influence and riff themes. It was in his soloists that Basie found his real strength, and many critics would say that their performances far outweighed the rather on-off standards of the band as a whole. Basie's piano led a band in which the soloists were definitely given their head, possibly to an even greater extent than were Ellington's stars. For Ellington not only indicated in his scores just where the adlibbing should come, but even inserted harmonic chords to guide his solo artists along lines that, however improvised, still fitted neatly into the essential flavour of the piece. Basie's freer ranging artists were paradoxically aided by racial prejudice. The very fact that they gained relatively low exposure even at their late Thirties peak, meant that without the pressure of playing commercial and crowd-pleasing music, they could really let themselves go. Not only that but the Count himself was hardly noted for his iron rule, even if in 1940 his patience with an errant Lester Young collapsed and the great sax player was fired for indiscipline.

Jimmie Lunceford, the third of the major black leaders of the Thirties, fell into the pattern of black bands of the time. Brilliant, but inconsistent, is the verdict often passed on this highly talented musician whose musical education was helped by Wilberforce J. Whiteman, Paul Whiteman's father. Duke Ellington may have been multiply talented in the various fields of band leading, but Lunceford's musical abilities were outstanding. He could play all the varieties of saxophone as well as flute and guitar. In addition to this he was, unlike Count Basie, an astute businessman, and could boast a Bachelor of Music Degree from Fisk University in Colorado.

After a time as a music teacher in Manssa High School in Memphis, and an up and down career playing in a campus band alongside Willie Smith, Edwin Wilcox and Henry Wells, all Fisk alumni, he finally moved to New York in 1933. The Lunceford Band, based around the style of Wilcox and Smith, and with a definite influence from leading arranger Sy Oliver who also played a major role in Tommy Dorsey's success, reached its peak from 1937-41. At its best Lunceford's band was a superb orchestral unit based around jazz as its musical foundation. The classical musical education of its major players undoubtedly gave it a special flavour all its own and one which, when combined with the arranging talents of a Swing creator like Oliver, rivalled all the great units of the time.

Inevitably Jimmie Lunceford's band came up against the unavoidable limitations of their blackness. They didn't get the exposure, the money or the fame that white contemporaries were showered with by zealous fans. Nonetheless one famous occasion does serve to prove how good the band really was, and how a discerning audience, black or white, could indeed appreciate true class. On November 18th, 1940 no less than twenty-eight top Swing outfits gathered in an epic Battle of the Bands at New York's Manhattan Centre. On stage for their allotted 15 minute sets apiece marched the star lineups of such leaders as Benny Goodman, Glenn Miller, Count Basie, Les Brown, Guy Lombardo and a whole lineup of the best in Swing. Of all the twenty-eight, every band arrived, played its 15 minutes, then left the stage, with one exception: Jimmie Lunceford's Band was not allowed to leave the stage by delirious fans until they had played several encores. There was no denying it, the band could certainly swing! The tragedy of Lunceford's leadership was that while he found the best musicians, more often than not he couldn't hang on to them. Living rough on the road and in the third rate hotels which were sometimes all that a black band could find open to them, wasn't the ideal life. And Lunceford's disciplined leadership, the product of his days as a music teacher, didn't mean that his band gained any more residencies. Despite a stopover at the Cotton Club in 1933 and short stays at places like the Fiesta Danceteria (1940) in Times Square, New York, the Lunceford Band spent far more time touring than not. Inevitably this affected their performance. Life on the road, even for the privileged elite of the top white bands, was never a picnic. For Jimmie Lunceford's Band it was obviously a nightmare. It was not surprising that Lunceford himself died of a heart attack in 1947. Naturally the band was on tour, this last time for Lunceford, in Oregon.

Prophets, as the saying goes, are never recognised in their own lands, and so it was for the great black bands of the Swing era. With a few exceptions, like Cab Calloway who managed to keep his outfit in a style envied by whites as well as blacks, life for the black musicians of the Thirties and Forties was tough and unfairly limited by a predominantly racist society. The enormous acclaim which came to black musicians in the rock music era was never theirs, however much the cognoscenti appreciated the best when they heard it. It seemed almost as if a band's musical creativity worked in inverse ratio to its nation-wide popularity. Even Duke Ellington found himself tied down by American racism. Certainly the man who hobnobbed with the British Royal Family when he toured their country wouldn't have found himself so welcome at President Roosevelt's White House.

Still the black musicians remained the innovators, from Fletcher Henderson onwards. And when in 1941 the rebels at Minton's Playhouse on 118th Street developed the weird new style they called 'bop' or 'rebop', naturally enough they were once again blacks. The problem was, and remains, that the big public for the most part don't really care about innovators. Benny Goodman's launch of Swing in the Palomar Ballroom in 1935 was an innovative as most people wanted to hear. If his music had been going the rounds through other musicians for five and ten years, that was as may be. That he escaped from the sweet sounds that had sugared the bitter pill of the Depression was sufficient. Ironically enough in the years after the great collapse of the big bands that followed the War, among the most feted survivors were the Basie and Ellington outfits, though in the case of the former the personnel was for a while cut radically. But then, as was pointed out in the case of Jimmie Lunceford's plaudits at the 1940 Battle of the Bands—class, come what may, does tell.

Jimmie Lunceford (*ABOVE*) and Jimmy Rushing (*BELOW*) were two of Swing's greatest, most talented showmen. Lunceford's background as an athletic coach gave him the discipline that forged a great band. Sy Oliver arranged, Willie Smith and Joe Thomas played and the fans lauded the swinging 'Lunceford two-beat'. Count Basie's standout blues shouter Jimmy Rushing, 'Mr Five By Five' was one more of the fluid, spontaneous talents that the Count assembled in one of the all-time great swing bands, black or white. Nurtured, like Basie, by the Moten outfit in Kansas City, Rushing cut immortal tracks backed by Lester Young, Freddie Green, Herschel Evans and the other Basie stars.

Bing Crosby came out of Whiteman's 'Rhythm Boys' to set the style for solo stardom. He crooned—they swooned, and from then on every day was Christmas day for our Bing.

CHAPTER EIGHT

CROONERS AND CANARIES

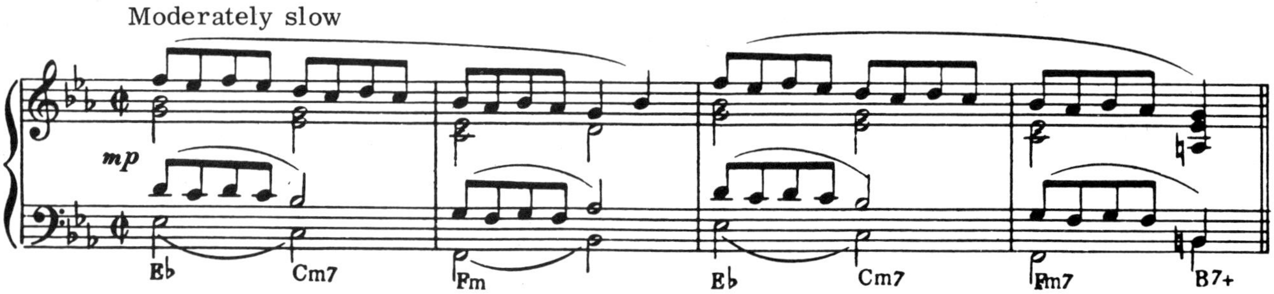

EVERY BAND, no matter what its musical style and public image, had one vital component in common: a vocalist. The leader might be, indeed usually was the real 'front man', but from the top names to the mickey-mouse outfits, there had to be a singer out there wowing and wooing the audience. Boy and girl vocalists, they were called, and often that was exactly what they were. Scared, but cocky teenagers, gleaned from a talent competition, or some nightclub where perhaps they were doubling as M.C. and occasional singer. On the wages sheets they were down as vocalists, but the audiences had their own, more pungent titles: Crooners and Canaries.

Despite the seemingly endless ranks of featured singers that Swing bands were parading at the height of their popularity, the concept of the star vocalist is a relatively recent invention. With very few exceptions, and excluding the rock scene, the majority of topline solo artists of today found their first success singing in front of one of the big bands of the Thirties and Forties.

Naturally there had always been singing acts of one sort or another. The vaudeville circuits were full of them. But as far as band vocalists were concerned, much of the credit for introducing this new attraction must go to Paul Whiteman. Whatever Whiteman's shortcomings may have been as a musician, there was no denying him his abilities as an innovator. When he picked up a singing act from Los Angeles and teamed them with a third voice under the name 'The Rhythm Boys' in 1926 he gave the world one of its most enduring star soloists: Bing Crosby. With Al Rinker, his partner in L.A. and Whiteman's Harry Barris, Crosby spearheaded the rise of the vocalist with the swing era bands. Whiteman didn't stop at the crooners either. Three years after putting the Rhythm Boys together Whiteman found the throbbing-voiced Mildred Bailey plugging songs behind a music counter in Seattle. He signed her up and launched the career of the first ever white girl vocalist to make her name.

Whiteman's pioneering efforts still didn't guarantee a massive surge of singers into the world of the big bands. As the Depression hit the music business with the same ferocity as it savaged the rest of the country, many units were forced to take cover for the duration rather than start moving in new directions. Much of the recording managed at the time was by random pick-up bands put together just to back one artist or another. Thus one finds Crosby putting out sides with help from the Dorsey Brothers, among others, and Bessie Smith fronting a collection that included Jack Teagarden and Benny Goodman. Leaders weren't above vocalising themselves around the Depression years, but their efforts, for instance those of Ben Pollack whose real talents lay in his drumming, were usually lamentable. Later on, when Swing was at its height, there were certain bands whose leaders doubled as singers—Little Jack Little, Skinnay Ennis, Will Osborne and others—but the really great vocalists never made that mistake. The roles, each vital, were not interchangeable. At least not on a successful level.

With the flowering of the Swing Era in the mid-Thirties, this dearth of top singers with big bands was over. By 1940, when Swing was peaking across America, the roll-call of crooners and canaries featured names that are today household words. Frank Sinatra with Tommy Dorsey, Perry Como with Ted Weems, Jimmy Rushing with Count Basie, Ella Fitzgerald with Chick Webb, Peggy Lee with Benny Goodman, Doris Day with Les Brown . . . the list is endless. Of all the great soloists of today, only Bing Crosby—who started out with a band—the late Nat Cole and Dinah Shore were not associated with one of the great Swing units of those days.

The role of the singers was very simple: he or she provided the best way of bringing the musicians and their product as close as possible to the audiences who came to hear them. Their songs were a vital link between the bandstand and the auditorium. And they provided, as did the star leaders, a definitely personal side to the band that helped the public identify with the unit as a whole. It was much more simple to relate one's enthusiasms to a featured artist, especially if that artist was singing rather than playing, than it was to pick up on a whole mass of musicians. Of course many fans didn't need this encouragement to support the band and enjoy their music, but the most cursory glance at the hysteria and excitement caused by Frank Sinatra or Bob Eberly makes it very clear just how good a job these singers did for their musicians.

If the ideal role of the crooner was simple, there was no certainty that life in the band would be that predictable. So much of what

Three of the best. Lee Brown's Doris Day (*ABOVE*), Chick Webb's Ella Fitzgerald (*TOP*) and Tommy Dorsey's still youthful Frank Sinatra (*FACING PAGE*). It took the big bands to set the songsters on their way, but the bandstands were soon only launching pads. Crises in the business, and the demands of war wrecked the bands. The singers just grabbed the limelight.

happened to the vocalist depended on his or her leader. No two leaders were alike, and the ups and downs of a singing career undoubtedly hinged on the leader and his personal style. One man would do everything in his power to help the singer, sometimes to the extent of subordinating the overall musical output to him or her, while another would use the singer merely as a useful but by no means exceptional appendage to the band. Some leaders were sympathetic, others were not—singers could only hope for the best. The contrasting careers of two of them, Bob Eberly (he changed the last letter out of personal choice) and his brother Ray Eberle provide a perfect illustration of how much the vocalist depended on the leader.

Jimmy Dorsey's boy vocalist Bob Eberly was discovered in the traditional manner: When the short-lived Dorsey Brothers' Band was playing a one-nighter in Troy, N.Y., they heard a singer who had won 'Allen's Amateur Hour', a radio talent show run by Fred Allen. Bob Eberly had done some singing around Troy, and also played a little four-string guitar. The Band were looking for a singer to replace Bob Crosby (Bing's brother who was never really in the first line of vocalists). Eberly was hired and when the Dorseys split he stayed with Jimmy.

Dorsey had the sense to realise that their talented vocalist could only benefit the band. When they won a spot on Bing Crosby's 'Kraft Music Hall', a radio show broadcast from Hollywood, he started to feature Eberly and to gear much of his music to the singer. By 1939 Eberly was able to rate second only to the perennial Bing Crosby in the annual *Metronome* popularity poll. His 527 votes were 100 behind his idol Crosby, upon whose style he unashamedly based his own signing, but left other top crooners in the shade. Tommy Dorsey's star attraction, Frank Sinatra, polled but 21 votes that year!

Where Bob Eberly really starred was in his famous duets with Jimmy Dorsey's girl vocalist Helen O'Connell who was hired for the band in 1939 after being discovered singing with Larry Funk's Band of a Thousand Memories in New York's Greenwich village. Top of the female singers' poll in 1940, Helen started off singing solos with the band—from novelties to torch songs—but was linked with Eberly after the Jimmy Dorsey Band picked up a three minute spot on another radio show, sponsored by 20 Grand Cigarettes. The popular arranger Tutti Camarata put together a slick act for the two star singers and the public loved it. Bob would start off singing a ballad, then an up-tempo jazz section would feature Jimmy on sax and the piece would be rounded of with Helen joining in for the final third, more of Bob's slow ballad. That Helen's limited vocal range kept her out of singing many of the trickier notes and left them to her partner didn't matter at all—it merely contributed to the very popular effect. The first record of the Eberly-O'Connell duets, 'Green Eyes', sold over 90,000 copies in the first few days after release. It was a spectacular testimony both to their abilities and to Jimmy Dorsey's prudence in letting his stars show their true class.

The relationship between Bob Eberly and Jimmy Dorsey was, in fact, exemplary. They formed a close friendship, shared apartments and generally promoted each other's virtues and abilities on and off the bandstand. When

BELOW: Bing Crosby entertains on radio's 'Stage Door Canteen'. All the classics you loved to hear, and plenty more besides.

lucrative offers arrived for Eberly (promoter Lou Levy offered him $100,000 to go solo, Paramount Pictures had plans for him to replace Dick Powell as a romantic star, and so on) there was never any question in the singer's mind: every offer was rejected without hesitation. No doubt this loyalty was not wholly altruistic. Dorsey's biggest hits, 'Marie Elena', 'I'm Glad There Is You', 'I Understand' and others, invariably rest almost wholly on Eberly for their impact and their popularity. Undoubtedly he provided the number one challenge to Frank Sinatra, and indeed, it was rumours of Eberly's possible launching of a solo career that broke Sinatra's ties with Tommy Dorsey in 1942; Sinatra was terrified lest his rival upstage him as a solo. Yet Eberly was not making a fortune out of Dorsey by any means. $400 per week with a $1,250 bonus for movies was no great shakes. Nevertheless right up until his entry into the U.S. Army in 1943 Bob Eberly remained loyal to Jimmy Dorsey.

The career of his brother Ray Eberle, who sang for Glenn Miller from 1938 to 1941 shows the other side of the coin. The same, in fact, goes for Miller's girl vocalist of that era, Marion Hutton whose career, while relatively successful, never really brought her the stardom attained by any of the really great Swing band ladies. While Glenn Miller's band was streets ahead of any other in overall popularity, its leader seemed to have some kind of block when it came to choosing singers. The way he picked up both Eberle and Hutton gives a telling insight to his stubborn untainted faith in his own opinions.

Frank Sinatra (*BELOW*) picks up his latest radio partner, sixteen-year-old Jane Powell. But Old Blue Eyes sang solo parts best.

In both cases it was obvious that Miller picked the loser of a two-horse race. Bob Eberly was widely rated as a great singer, but Miller was always convinced that brother Ray was the superior singer. In the same way, Marion Hutton's sister Betty had the votes, but Glenn Miller chose sister Marion despite innumerable contrary opinions. Eberle, hired without any professional experience, but quite simply because he was Bob Eberly's brother, never really made it big. Many critics of Miller's performances admitted openly that Ray was dragging the musical standard of the band below its true potential, and this didn't help the singer himself. But he was Miller's favourite, for a while anyway, and that was that. The same went for Marion Hutton. The epitome of the sweet hometown girl, Marion could make girl scouts look brassy, but her sweetness didn't make her a singer. Once again, she was Miller's pet, relating to him more as a daughter than as a professional employee, and there was nothing anyone could do about it. No doubt the malleable duo were ideal for Miller's autocratic personality. He could mould his singers in the image he wanted and not worry about their running away with their own importance. Of all the bands, Miller's was the greatest in the Swing Era, yet none of his singers had a post-Swing career of the magnitude of the vocalists from lesser units.

Much of the weakness of Miller's singers came from Miller's own style. While Dorsey might encourage his singers, and actually put his music second to them, Glenn Miller put music first and foremost. The musicians played the song and it was up to the vocalists to adapt as best they might. Obviously this wasn't a style exclusively Glenn Miller's. Other bands had autocratic leaders—Artie Shaw and

Sincerely
Kay Starr
Capitol
REG. U.S. PAT. OFF.
RECORDS

Benny Goodman were equally obsessed with musical perfection above all—but as far as the singers were concerned, it was no help. No wonder, then, that songs with a Ray Eberle or Marion Hutton vocal languished on the shelves while the public bought versions by lesser bands with more exciting vocalists.

Eberle and Hutton may have been Glenn Miller's favourites, but that didn't help their lives in the band particularly. Eberle turned to drink on occasion and the naturally nervous Marion Hutton sometimes found the hectic pace too much. One night during the record-breaking Glen Island Casino performances of 1939 she collapsed on the stand; her place was temporarily filled by Kay Starr, a fledgling canary. Marion even quit the band for a while in 1941 when a gossip columnist printed that Marion, quite legitimately married to Jack Philbin, was pregnant. Embarrassed by the report she quit the band, though came back to sing with Miller for the last few months of his peacetime performing. Even then, her temperament betrayed her at the final Miller gig in Passaic, N.J., when she broke down in tears on stage and rushed away, overcome with the emotion of Miller's farewell show.

Ray Eberle's departure from the band was equally emotional, but less palatable for all concerned. He was summarily fired by Miller after an incident which was never satisfactorily explained and still has its partisan views. In a *Metronome* interview Eberle claimed Miller was too despotic in his treatment of his artists and that he, Eberle, had not been paid for performing in the film 'Orchestra Wives'. Miller on the other hand said that Eberle had been too drunk to appear on stage. The truth of the matter lies between the two, although Eberle's late arrival at that night's show in Chicago was actually caused by a traffic snarl-up. As far as payment was concerned, Eberle was right, but then his contract with Miller had never mentioned movie bonuses anyway. It was an unhappy incident and casts an unfavourable light on both parties. But for Miller discipline came first, and shrewd business sense shortly after. Ray Eberle or not, the Glenn Miller Orchestra was still topping every poll.

Most of the crooners and canaries of the Swing Era fell somewhere between the extremes of Bob Eberly and Ray Eberle or their female equivalents. While unique talents, such as those of Frank Sinatra or Perry Como might be recognised and indulged, the bands for whom they sang were essentially dance bands and as such had no particular obligation to keep the vocalists happy. As Glenn Miller proved, singers weren't vital for success. Nonetheless, the mob hysteria that greeted such stars as Sinatra proved that to ignore that kind of talent was absurd. Why not capitalise on the available stars, whether in the band or at the mike? If a singer like Ella Fitzgerald could bring a band real prominence, as she did for Chick Webb with her recording of 'A-Tisket A-Tasket', no sensible leader would ignore the potential he had unearthed.

Looking back at the young singers of the Swing Era, they are on the whole a clean-cut, All-American bunch. Obviously there were exceptions, but for every Anita O'Day whose gutsy style complimented the wild drumming of her leader Gene Krupa, there were a score of Marion Hutton girls-next-door. The average vocalist came from the right side of the tracks and had no intention of crossing them. The rewards, of course, were enormous, but for the run of the mill singers, life in the big bands wasn't especially glamorous or comfortable. Apart from the extent to which success or failure depended, as has been noted above, on the whims and idiosyncrasies of a particular leader, there were other imponderables to be faced. Today's rock bands travel in airplanes or limousines; the big bands of the Swing Era had no such luxury. The usual mode of transport was a large bus. Sometimes a special train was chartered, but this luxury tended to appear for more subtle reasons than giving the musicians ease and comfort. Black bands, whose skin colour caused trouble on tours of the South and who might be refused accommodation in many segregationalist hotels, found it easiest to avoid friction by hiring a train, complete with sleeping cars, to keep them out of troubles of that sort.

Bob Eberly, and others of his status, might be pulling in $400 per week, as well as healthy bonuses for filming with the band, but more likely than not the vocalists' real rank was reflected in a pay packet substantially smaller

Perry Como (*ABOVE*) and Peggy Lee (*BELOW*) learnt everything from their big band days with Ted Weems and Benny Goodman. Come the new era, they would reap the massive rewards.

than that of the musicians. Ray Eberle was paid a mere $35 by Miller when he was hired, some $15 less than the musicians. Out of these wages vocalists, and musicians for that matter, were supposed to pay for their own accommodation, food, laundry bills and so on. There was no effective union and it was not until 1938 that bands worked anything less than a seven-day week. No doubt the leaders worked just as hard, but they, unlike many of the musicians, particularly the mass of unfeatured sidemen, as well as the unspectacular, workaday singers, were pulling in a substantial share of the profits. Life in the bands was hard, no matter who you were, and public acclaim and high wages only partially made up for daily show-to-show hops of up to 500 miles. Not until the war was the daily move restricted to a slightly more reasonable 300 miles. No wonder musicians and singers collapsed or hit the bottle in an attempt to keep themselves on top. Artie Shaw, who as a successful leader had the best of the big band life, still found the pressure too much and quite simply dropped all his commitments and fled to Mexico in 1938. The Mid-West solidity of Glenn Miller and other tough disciplinary leaders may have lacked verve, but they stood up under pressure better than did more temperamental figures.

When the Swing Era began the average singer always needed a band as a vehicle for his or her talents. But as it progressed and the boy and girl vocalists matured both in years and in talents their popularity soared and it didn't take any great genius to realise that in many cases the singers were becoming the main attraction. The perfect case in point was the young vocalist with Tommy Dorsey's Band—Frank Sinatra. Sinatra had started out as a singing M.C. at the Rustic Inn in Englewood, N.J., and had the luck to be heard on a radio show from the Inn by band leader Harry James. James rushed up to Englewood, expecting to find the singer he had heard working with a band, but discovered that Sinatra was unattached. He hired the young singer forthwith and actually asked him to change his name. Sinatra refused. It was at a gig at the Sherman Hotel in Chicago that Sinatra was heard by Tommy Dorsey, on the lookout for a singer to replace Jack Leonard who had just

Nat 'King' Cole (*ABOVE*) avoided the big bands, but still made their essence his own. Having played in small combos, he found the transition to singing solo later in his life an easy one. Billie Holiday (*TOP*), with Barney Bigard and Louis Armstrong, struggled alone, but put in some gigs with Artie Shaw. Al Rinker (*INSET CENTRE*) sang with Crosby in Whiteman's Rhythm Boys, while those curvaceous canaries Jo Stafford (*INSET LEFT*) and Anita O'Day (*RIGHT INSET*) trilled for Tommy Dorsey and Gene Krupa.

quit. Sinatra's wife Nancy was pregnant, Dorsey was offering more money, and Harry James decided not to stand in the singer's way. Sinatra changed hands, and with that change, moved from being just another (talented) singer, towards becoming the monumental star of the mid-Forties and afterwards.

Tommy Dorsey was no carbon copy of his brother Jimmy who quite happily subordinated his band to the vocal abilities of Bob Eberly and Helen O'Connell. But he was no fool either. Sinatra's debut at the Lyric Theatre in Indianapolis brought the house down, even though the young singer had only prepared two songs and had to fake his way through a rapturously received encore. Dorsey knew he had a winner.

The point of Sinatra's relationship with Tommy Dorsey was that they were mutually useful. Dorsey's band was neither a vehicle for Sinatra, nor was Sinatra merely a prop for the band. As the one progressed from strength to strength, so, too, did the other. Sinatra was perfect at projecting Dorsey's image as 'The Sentimental Gentleman of Swing' and as he helped Dorsey by blending with his music, so did he help himself. He worked in tandem with canary Jo Stafford and a male back-up trio known as the Pied Pipers. By 1941 there was never any doubt that Tommy Dorsey could boast the best vocal lineup in the country.

Inevitably Frank Sinatra had to move on. His contract to Dorsey, in line with the contracts of many performers in Swing Era bands, gave an enormous proportion of his earnings to the leader, but even this failed to deter him. Eventually, anyway, he was able to buy his way out with help from his agency and various concerned friends. In 1942, faced by rumours that Bob Eberly, his number one rival, was about to go solo, Sinatra quit Dorsey. From thereon in, Sinatra's career bloomed and blossomed. As they say, the rest is musical history.

Sinatra's bid for solo stardom was no more than a precedent for other big band vocalists. The great mass, no doubt, had no option but to stay with their parent bands, but for the stars whose public acclaim was so obviously rivalling and sometimes even outdoing that of the bands with which they sang, there was a growing temptation to go it alone. And few were as

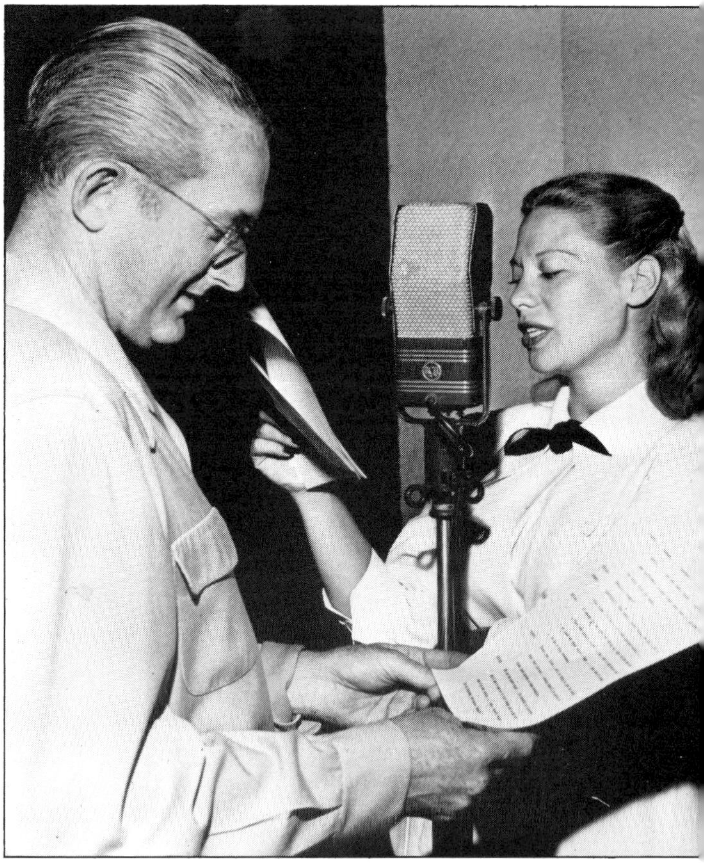

ABOVE: **After the ball was over – Tommy Dorsey interviews Dinah Shore on his post-war television series, thanks to Jackie Gleason.**

ABOVE: **Hunchbacked black drummer Chick Webb kept things swinging up in Harlem's Savoy Ballroom. He could wipe the floor with Krupa anytime, and his songbird Ella Fitzgerald ruled the vocal roost, the charm of her emotive voice moving millions.**

ABOVE: The entire Chick Webb band, showing in centre stage their starring attraction, the elegant first lady of song, Ella Fitzgerald. She joined the band in mid-1935 after having been discovered singing in an amateur talent contest in the Harlem Opera House.

devoted to their leader as was Bob Eberly. When the fight between the Musicians Union and recording companies halted big band action in the studios on August 1st, 1942,the reins were finally loosed. The bands had been weakened by the draft which took their musicians off to the war; the recording ban was another savage blow to their continued success. For vocalists the recording ban had a minimal effect. They didn't need vast orchestration to put songs onto wax or acetate. As the bands gradually slumped under the pressure, the singers grew stronger and more popular. By the end of the band and the end of the war, solo artists were the rage, not the big bands. That almost without exception these solo stars had been discovered and nurtured by the Swing bands made no difference. They would survive where the bands would go under. That someone like Bob Eberly has not kept up with the big solo names of today is no doubt part due to his loyalty to Jimmy Dorsey. While Sinatra, Perry Como and others were tasting the fruits of individual acclaim that had seemed in the Thirties to be the personal property of Bing Crosby, Eberly had served out his war with Wayne King's band in Chicago, a Senior Citizens' favourite and a far cry from Dorsey. When he came back he auditioned for a spot on the Chesterfield Supper Club. Practically and symbolically he lost the gig to Perry Como.

For a while, in the post-war euphoria, the big bands had a final flourish, but it was belated glory. The public taste had been given a new look, and vocalists were in. For those who didn't like singers, there had been other changes: the rebels at Minton's with their 'bop' playing had captured the avant-garde. Where stages had once been packed with musicians, now there was need only for the solo artist out there in the spotlight. Naturally they still had their accompaniment, but those bands which kept going were there strictly in the secondary spot. The Swing Era bands may well have been unable to appear without a singer, but for the crooners and the canaries they had reared, there was no need for a band. The birds had flown the nest.

After a while it was just one long barrage of telephone numbers as Miller's chart busting band reached new highs in the esteem of the dance-hungry, toe-tapping public. The band would swing to the cash till's ring.

CHAPTER NINE

STRINGS OF PEARLS

BY 1940 the Glenn Miller Orchestra could do no wrong. They weren't the swingingest band on the block, but then they didn't pretend to be. And if the kind of nationwide response they were getting meant anything, then they didn't need to be, either. For a band which, only a year before, had been playing third-rate tourist joints at a cut fee just for the radio exposure and a look at the Great White Way, Glenn Miller's outfit had come a long way. Some times it must have been hard to remember the bad old days. Success breeds success; the truism worked fine for Miller and his band. The toughest problem they had to face by the start of the new decade was just how in hell to fit in all the gigs, concerts and radio shows. Apart from that, if you forget the problems of income tax—something that Miller had never had to consider before—it was laughs all the way.

1939 ended in a slew of packed houses. The band found their first major radio slot with regular appearances on Lucky Strike cigarettes 'Lucky Strike Hit Parade'. They were elected, though veritable Johnnys-Come-Lately, as one of four bands that ASCAP (American Society of Composers, Artists and Performers) put into Carnegie Hall for an 'All-Time Greats' line-up. The rest of the bill featured Benny Goodman, Paul Whiteman and Fred Waring. They played another session at Frank Dailey's Meadowbrook, with a generous pay hike. Now the musicians were getting an average of $75 a week, with around a hundred dollars for the section leaders and the solo stars. There was also an important addition to the band. Late 1938 Artie Shaw had walked petulantly off the stand and told his band, 'You have it, boys'. He'd left one of the top bands in Swing without a leader while he skipped to Mexico to recuperate. There were sidemen going begging. Miller, ever astute, picked up one of the best—Jerry Gray, Shaw's top ranking arranger. Miller always preferred Gray to his other arranger, Bill Finegan. Gray, as far as the boss was concerned, was more disciplined, looked for tighter, more rigid forms. Just what the maestro ordered, in fact. Paradoxically, Jerry Gray was never that happy with the Miller set-up, though he stayed on. He longed for the free and easy swinging sound that he'd been producing for Artie Shaw. But while he was with Miller he created some of the Orchestra's greatest hits. 'Sun Valley Jump', 'Pennsylvania 6-5000' and 'A String of Pearls' were all Jerry Gray originals.

'Pennsylvania 6-5000' as every Miller fan knew, was the telephone number of the Hotel

Pennsylvania in New York where the band started a three month residency in January 1940. They went back twice again before Glenn went to Europe and the Hotel's Cafe Rouge became, if anywhere could claim the honour, the musical home of the Glenn Miller Orchestra.

There was another claimant to that position that ought to be considered. Miller's residencies at the Hotel Pennsylvania certainly dragged in his New York fans, but another show, that lasted from 1940 right through to his final concert in September 1942 went out for the listening pleasure of everyone who tuned into the CBS network on Tuesdays, Wednesdays and Thursdays. 'Are you smoking the cigarette that satisfies,' insinuated the announcer, and another thrice-weekly airing of the Chesterfield cigarettes 'Moonlight Serenade' show was on the air. Glenn Miller for fifteen solid minutes. Well, not quite, For the first thirteen weeks of the show Miller was sharing the spotlight with Patti, Maxene and Laverne, the singing Andrews Sisters. They had their three minute slot, Miller had another nine and of course the sponsor grabbed three prime time minutes to boost the product across America. Miller and the Sisters always got on tolerably; it was the feuding and fighting between the girls that set the problem off. They weren't happy with three minutes anyway and after a mere three months the show was all Miller's.

During the first few months of 1940 the Orchestra was meeting pressures that most of the musicians had probably never believed existed. There were the supper and dinner sets at the Café Rouge; there were the three times a week Chesterfield shows, with three rehearsals to go with them. And there was a strenuous recording programme for RCA Victor.'Tuxedo Junction', a simple riff number that Miller had heard Erskine Hawkins playing up in Harlem's Savoy Ballroom hadn't really turned on any of the band. Except for Glenn himself. He had an arrangement put together and went into the studio. The single sold 115,000 copies in the first week! On top of all this Miller was still appearing at the Paramount Theatre for three dozen shows a week. All in all the band was playing 54 sets a

ABOVE: "Chesterfields . . . make a real trombonist of you." Miller was in a nicotine nirvana as the sponsors' cash flowed in.

ABOVE: Eddie Sauter and Bill Finegan arranged for Goodman and Miller. Later their own band was to wow the Fifties.

ABOVE: **Perfectionist Fred Waring was a veteran disciplinarian. He started off as a dance band boss but soon formed his 'Glee Club', concentrating on the vocals. He drove his singers, like Donna Dee and Gordon Goodman (*INSETS*) harder than maybe they liked.**

week. It was an enormous output and one which would not be tolerated, or even proposed today. Not surprisingly the pressure bore down on Miller and he actually collapsed. His fellow leaders rallied round and while Glenn did miss a few Paramount sets, a couple of days at the Café Rouge and the only 'Moonlight Serenade' programme he was ever absent from, men like Tommy Dorsey, Gene Krupa and Charlie Barnet filled in loyally.

On April 4th the band closed at the Café Rouge. With a $2,000 a week guarantee secure, Miller had never failed to exceed it for all fourteen weeks the band played that room. His lowest pay for a week was $2,030 and it rose to a peak of $3,054. Not bad at all for a bandleader who would have probably paid money for the exposure a Cafe Rouge residency would have brought him a year before. That kind of money, as was mentioned above, did have some drawbacks. Miller's income tax had never cost him more than six measly dollars up until 1939. That year the IRS claims hit $200. But from now on, Glenn Miller was well aware that his earnings would be worth far more to his country's taxmen. He was advised by tax lawyers to move across from New York to New Jersey. His office became based in Tenafly, N.J. and he bought a house there for Helen and himself to enjoy during his rare moments of freedom. In April, to celebrate the success of the Cafe Rouge engagement, the band issued 'Pennsylvania 6-5000'. It sold a substantial 40,000 copies in the first week. Just in case there were still any doubts on the matter, the latest WNEW poll put Miller at the very top of the New York band pops. And, perhaps fittingly for a man whose confidence had sometimes suffered over the years, he was sent a personal letter of congratulation from no less an All-American luminary as Dale Carnegie. Miller, it appeared, had indeed made friends and influenced people. Or, in the words of modern Carnegie ads, the Glenn Miller Orchestra had certainly maximised its potential.

Winning the WNEW poll in summer 1940 showed just how far ahead of the competition Miller had come. His votes totalled 44,446. His nearest rival, Tommy Dorsey, could only manage 23,645 and Benny Goodman, the number three man, limped in with

ABOVE: **Poor Marion Hutton never really made the grade. Still Miller, steadfastly following the middle path, loved her. She was his all-American girl-next-door. Fortunately for her, outstanding solo talent was never a quality vital to the band's musical stance.**

16,321. It just underlined the Miller supremacy. As far as the leader was concerned there was only one person in 1940 who made him jealous: Kay Kyser, whose band, with its gimmickry and blatant commercialism, made no bones about going for the sweeter side of the street. When orchestra takes were totted up at the end of the year, Miller had grossed a nifty $700,000; only Kyser, with a cool million bucks, had the edge on him. Of that seven hundred thousand, Glenn Miller's own takehome pay—before the tax people got stuck into it—was some $26,750. His wife Helen also came in for $9,000 that year. The band wages came to $232,442 and the rest went to managers, agents, bookers and all the other running costs a big band incurred.

Like all the best swing band leaders, Glenn Miller was a businessman. And as a businessman he was continually irked by the poor fees and non-existent royalties that a recording band could command. It was fine to see the exposure and popularity that a big seller like 'Tuxedo Junction' or 'Pennsylvania 6-5000' could bring the band, but where was all the money those records were bringing in? To counter this problem Miller founded the Mutual Music Society—his own publishing company which included amongst its directors Helen Miller, who pulled in a comfortable six hundred dollars a month to take care of housekeeping. With his own publishing company to take care of his band's recording and sheet music output, Miller gave a big boost to the annual income. Now he was in line for the royalty that ASCAP paid on every radio play, and of course the big record companies were duty bound to deliver publishing royalties even if they hadn't yet been forced to hand over performing ones.

Miller's business acumen suffered slightly in the ASCAP-BMI (Broadcast Music Inc.) war that hit the industry in January 1941. Until it ended in October of the same year, nobody who had registered his records under ASCAP was able to take advantage of radio airplay. ASCAP had demanded even more money from the radio companies as royalties for airplay, and the radio companies with their own BMI registry, retaliated by boycotting all ASCAP material. While Miller's company was BMI affiliated, many of his great early hits were under the ASCAP banner. 'Moonlight Serenade' itself was thus unavailable for a theme tune and the Chesterfield show was temporarily set off with something called 'Slumber Song'. Other banned hits included 'Tuxedo Junction', 'In the Mood' and 'Pennsylvania 6-5000'. It was a nuisance, but the overall Miller popularity was untouched. After all, the ASCAP boycotting affected all the bands equally.

ABOVE: **The Modernaires, four toothsome songsters, put a little pep into the Miller vocal lineup. They peaked with 'Chattanooga Choo-Choo', but generally improved the thin Eberle-Hutton voice-overs.**

The 1941 Miller story just sees the bandwagon rolling along. 1940 had ended in triumph at the Battle of the Bands at the Manhattan Centre. 6,000 fans packed the hall as no less than twenty-eight bands played consecutive fifteen minute sets from eight in the evening all the way through till four the next morning. Only one band received an encore, and that was Jimmie Lunceford's exquisite combo, but with the exception of the black master, Miller's ovation topped Basie, Goodman, Lombardo, Kaye and all the rest. The fans' verdict was underlined when Miller topped the Sweet section of January's *Downbeat* poll.

The year opened with slight changes in the vocal side of the band. Marion Hutton, quite respectably married to music publisher Jack Philbin, was pregnant. It didn't worry her particularly until a gossip writer grabbed the story and tossed it over to the public. For reasons best known to the never-overconfident singer, the story was a great embarrassment and she resigned from the band. Her replacement was Dorothy Claire, who was snatched from the Bobby Byrne Band, thus starting a minor war between Miller and Byrne. But Dorothy didn't make the Miller grade and soon she was replaced by another canary, Paula Kelly. In the end, with her child safely born, Marion Hutton came back to the band, it was a great relief for all concerned.

The other change in the Miller vocals was the introduction of a male voice foursome, the Modernaires. The four singers, Chuck Goldstein, Hal Dickenson (who married Paula Kelly), Bill Conway and Ralph Brewster, had already achieved some reputation when they recorded the theme of Martin Block's 'Make Believe Ballroom' with a backing from Charlie Barnet's Band. Miller snapped them up for a ten-year management contract and paid them $125 a week a head. The most famous of the many Modernaires' recordings for the band was 'Chattanooga Choo Choo'. First off they sang this with Tex Beneke, whose vocal talents were quite often used to boost his abilities on the sax, but it was in Miller's film 'Sun Valley Serenade' that the song really came into its own as the Nicholas Brothers performed a breath-taking tap sequence against a railroad backdrop and the band's playing and the Modernaires' song.

The big band boom had reached the kind of peak in 1941 that meant it was right in line for America's supreme honour. the trip to Hollywood. In the event it was an honour that most of the bands could have done well without, although the high wages and easy living, not to mention a break from endless performances in hotels and theatres, must have provided a welcome relief. All the big bands were dragged out to the West Coast movie mecca one by one. The style had started when the new craze, Benny Goodman, was imported to Hollywood in the mid-Thirties and given a demanding role, along with his band, in a second-rater called 'Hollywood Hotel'. Next came Artie Shaw in 'Dancing Co-Ed' and soon the rush was on. If you were making it big on the Swing circuit, then off you had to trot to the celluloid city and get your (moving) picture taken. Few of the bands can have liked such garish, irrelevant and innacurate vehicles as 'Ball of Fire' (Gene Krupa), 'Las Vegas Nights' (Tommy Dorsey), 'The Gang's All Here' (Benny Goodman), or 'Swing Fever' (Kay Kyser). Neither were the massive dosages of 'Stage Door Canteen' (Basie, Cugat, Goodman, Kyser, Lombardo and Freddie Martin) or 'Jam Session' (Louis Armstrong, Barnet, Glen Gray, Jan Garber, Teddy Powell, Alvino Rey, and Jo Stafford and the Pied Pipers) any more calculated to make the right impression. Of course Hollywood had its uses for the bands. The American Federation of Musicians' strike was called in 1942 by James Petrillo, and if there was no recording, then big bands might as well pick up the odd dollar in the movie studios. Around 1942 some of the greatest bands of them all trekked out to the coast, to perform for the public and to make the odd movie. But few of the films ever did well and by 1944 the movie moguls had turned their interests and their chequebooks in a new direction.

Nevertheless, the Glenn Miller Orchestra, as one of the biggest of the big, had to make the obligatory trip out West and once there produce the necessary couple of flicks. 'Sun Valley Serenade' is no worse than any other band film, and some generous critics have even rated it better than most. With Miller in the role of bandleader 'Phil Corey', the film starred Sonia Henie and John Payne as the romantic leads, Milton Berle along for a laugh and extra parts for Dorothy Dandridge, Lynn Bari, Joan David and the black dancing duo, the Nicholas Brothers. Reviews said that Miller managed to make 'Phil Corey' a convincing figure. Whether Miller saw this as flattery is debatable. The movie was showcased at Hollywood's Paladium Ballroom and here Miller's celebrated refusal to miss out on a penny due to him caused some unpleasant friction. In the Hollywood tradition there was a mass of free tickets available to critics, celebrities, movie people and the like. Miller stepped in firmly: nobody, and that included his wife Helen, was getting in free to a show that was making money for Glenn Miller. 'The Unpleasantness of 1941' as the incident became known amongst the Miller entourage, was on a par with some of his most crass, puritanical gestures, akin to the enforced removal of the AAF Band's moustaches a couple of years later. When the second Miller film opened in 1942, there was a different venue. 'Orchestra Wives' (its title) and the real life

With Miller gone it was anyone's guess who got to pick up the pieces. Gordon 'Tex' Beneke (*ABOVE*) jumped quickest onto the still rolling bandwagon. The Boss' favourite, saxman Beneke, par for the Miller course, was never a top soloist. Ray McKinley had taken the band through France, but on civvy street Beneke got the big gig. His leadership echoed his playing: it never really made it. Don Haynes, another Miller intimate, was the real leader while Tex just moved further and further into making the musicians his personal band.

performing husbands who went with them, were *persona non grata* at the Palladium. This second Miller film was equally as distinguished, or as undistinguished—depending on the viewers' taste—as its predecessor. This time the hero was George Montgomery, a trumpeter whose music was played by Miller regular Johnny Best. Heroine was Ann Rutherford and this time Jackie Gleason provided what little comedy the film could muster. Reglars like Lynn Bari filled in and the musical hits were 'At Last', 'Serenade In Blue' and, most popular, 'I've Got a Gal in Kalamazoo'.

The war in Europe had begun just around the time in Autumn 1939 that Glenn Miller had released his all-time number one hit, 'Moonlight Serenade'. Now the more percipient American eyes were turning towards Europe and even though Roosevelt promised that 'never again will your boys become involved in a foreign war', the Government introduced the draft in early 1940. No-one in America was particularly keen to rush off to fight in Europe once again, but with draft boards claiming their victims across the country, nobody could forget the possibility.

The personnel of the big bands were as liable to conscription as the next guy. Miller's youngsters, specially picked because they were young and thus malleable under the Miller regime, were all eligible. Only Glenn Miller and Chummy Macgregor were officially out of the War—protected by the over 35 limit on conscription. As for the rest, trumpeter Ray Anthony was only 19 and thus only just scraped in at the other end of the eligibility lists. Others, like a great Miller favourite, bassman Herman 'Trigger' Alpert, drummer Moe Purtill and arranger Billy May were just 24, the perfect age for the draft. Ray Eberle was only 22 as was Jimmy Priddy. Second sax, Al Klink was 25. And so it went right through the band. All ripe for draft board plucking.

First to go was Alpert, who was snatched off to war even though Miller was able to get him a six month deferment. But the Government was inexorable. And so was the tide of war. Obviously all eyes were attuned, if anywhere, to events in Europe, and when the blow fell in the Far East only those in the know would have expected it, but as 1941 slipped away, the spectre of the war came closer all the time. And as a good All-American, at the head of a whole bunch of other All-Americans, Glenn Miller soon found that his patriotic instincts were pulling him towards some kind of war service.

On October 4th, 1941 Miller started up his personal gesture to the newly drafted troops. Playing from the bandstand of the Café Rouge at the Hotel Pennsylvania where the band had just opened their third residency since January 1940, Miller launched 'Sunset Serenade'. The programme format was simple, designed to bring in as many listeners as

Miller's movies, 'Sun Valley Serenade' (*ABOVE*) and 'Orchestra Wives' (*FACING PAGE*) were no worse than average Hollywood big band exploitation vehicles. The kinder critics even said they were above average. Miller knew better, but he never missed out on a few extra bucks, not to mention all that profitable publicity. And there was no masking the quality of Miller's music.

possible from the camps around the country, and simultaneously showing how the Glenn Miller Orchestra were doing their part. Five camps would be selected before each show and in each five a poll would be held for their favourite Miller number. During the show the band would play each while listeners phoned in to vote for their favourite of the five. The winning song would be announced and the camp who had selected it was sent a phonograph and fifty swing singles. Not all of them, it is worth noting, were Miller's own. These shows could prove costly. One time, just after the ASCAP-BMI war was over and 'Chattanooga Choo Choo' had been released for the first time, all five of the camps Miller had selected chose it in their polls. Sure enough, all five were sent their record player and bundle of records. The giveaways cost around $1,000 a show. Another gesture towards the war efforts was Miller's method of charging admission for his Café Rouge 'Sunset Serenade' shows. Everyone who came in had to buy US savings stamps which would then be sent along to the USO, an organisation dedicated to entertaining service men and women. This last gesture didn't endear Miller to the Hotel Pennsylvania staff. There were few orders and fewer tips from the kids who crowded, nearly fifteen hundred strong into a room designed for 400 basic and 625 at a squeeze. The numbers had, reluctantly, to be limited.

Miller swept into the new year with a quick three weeks back at the Paramount. He closed the Cafe Rouge in January—netting over $41,750 for the fourteen week gig—and in his three weeks at the Theatre took over $167,000. In February the Glenn Miller Orchestra won the WNEW poll yet again, something of a regular event by now, but in February Miller took a step infinitely more important to his band's career: he registered himself with Local Draft Board no. 7, in Bergen County, New Jersey. In June of that year he went to the Ninth Naval District and formally applied for a commission in the US Navy Reserve. Playing for the camps had been a gesture, but it was not the level of participation in the now open war effort that Miller

Pattie, Maxine and Laverne, the Andrews Sisters. Billed with Miller on the Chesterfield Show, all they created was trouble. Three weeks of squabbling and Miller was in the hot seat all alone.

wanted. Before Pearl Harbour it had been enough to send records, now Glenn Miller wanted to come along himself.

With one eye turned to a possible commission, Miller kept the other as firmly as ever on his current problems. Number one, as usual, was money. He had started a publishing company and recouped some missing revenue from that. Now he tried for even greater returns on his talent. In an attempt to increase his financial independance he tried to cut the fee he paid his booking agency GAC (formerly Rockwell-O'Keefe) from the usual 15% to a mere 5%. The agency was unimpressed. They retaliated by stopping all monies currently owing the band. When the case went to the Musicians Union for arbitration, the Union ruled in favour of the Agency. Miller had to pay over his fifteen per cent and like it.

Another setback came in August when to his immense surprise the Navy regretfully turned down his application for a commission. Quick to sense rejection, Miller at once was convinced that he was not good enough, too old and so on. But he was encouraged by friends to try again if that was what he really wanted. Like so many men of his age, in all the areas of war, Miller started writing to everyone he knew who might help him. Just like Evelyn Waugh's Guy Crouchback Miller went the rounds of all his military connections, looking for a way into active service. It might have been the irritation engendered by this frustrating summer that led to yet another unfortunate incident: the abrupt and unpleasant sacking of singer Ray Eberle. Whether, as Miller contended, Eberle was going over the top with his drinking, or whether, as Eberle claimed, Miller was just being his usual pig-headed self when he, Eberle, had to miss the start of a show through getting stuck in a traffic jam, is anybody's guess. One thing is clear—Eberle, chosen in the first place by Miller for reasons that were about as deeply considered as were those that saw him sacked, was never really that great a singer. The pace and style of the Miller band proved a challenge he couldn't tackle. Miller lavished affection and attention on him, but Eberle never came up to par. It was probably this, more than anything else, that put Ray Eberle in the hot seat that day in 1942.

On September 10, 1942 Miller's letter-writing paid off. Thanks to the pull exerted by one of his contacts, Brigadier-General Charles D. Young, Miller was to be inducted into the US Army and given a commission as Captain. He would, once in the Army and through his basic training, be set to work organising some form of music for the troops. Miller started planning at once. He saw infinite possibilities in the Army. As will be seen, he missed the infinite pitfalls.

As soon as the news came through, first to the band and then to the rest of the music business, Miller's sidemen were flooded with offers. All the members of the trombone section were snapped up by Charlie Spivak, whose band, along with that of Claude Thornhill had been backed initially by a combination of Miller's and Cy Shribman's money. Moe Purtill went back to Tommy Dorsey and replaced Buddy Rich; Skip Nelson, the singer who had replaced Ray Eberle, went back to the Ben Pollack band which was backing Chico Marx. Tex Beneke, Marion Hutton and the Modernaires went off round the country on a theatre tour of their own. Miller hoped that, on their being drafted, those of the band who wanted, would be able to join him in a service outfit.

Before everyone could go their separate ways, the Glenn Miller Orchestra still had a few more shows to do. The last one, and coincidentally the last of the Chesterfield Shows, was at the Central Theatre, Passaic, N.J. First of all Miller handed over his Chesterfield spot to Harry James. Then the band played out their civilian life to an audience of weeping fans. The kids wept, the band wept, Marion Hutton gave up to her emotions half way through 'Kalamazoo'. Historically, even the stoical leader, Glenn Miller himself, had to turn away from his audience and brush what just might have been a tear from his eye.

At the end of the show an hysterical audience cried for more. But that was it. The Glenn Miller Orchestra which had falterred for a couple of years and then strutted so proudly for three more, had played its last set. America's cannon fodder, plucked straight off those mid-western Main Streets, was off to the front, and Captain Glenn Miller, Main Street's favourite son, was going to do his bit.

Jimmy Stewart starred, the others only played the music. 'Glenn Miller Story' lineup from left to right. *Back row* — Trummy Young, Cosy Cole, Barney Bigard, Artell Shaw. *Front row* — Ben Pollack, Gene Krupa, Louis Armstrong, 'Glenn', Joe Yukl, Marty Napoleon.

CHAPTER TEN

THE MILLER MYTHS

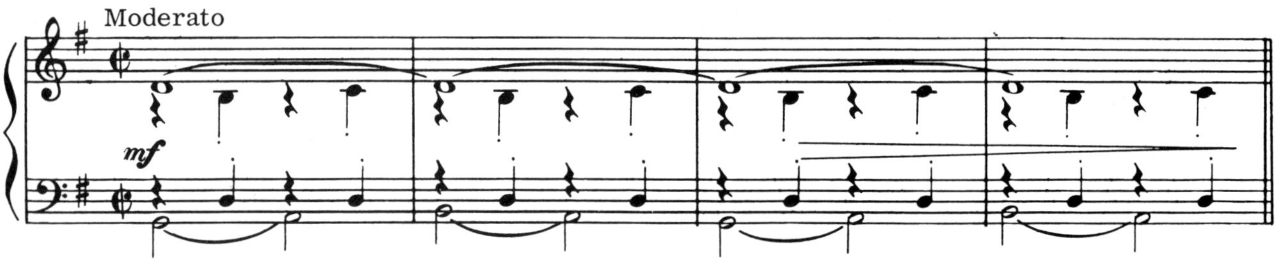

TWO ANECDOTES from the many will serve. Leading the AAF Band sometime during the war, Miller suddenly turned to the assembled musicians and demanded that all moustaches should be shorn. There was no reason for this, other than his opinion that they looked 'too much like gangsters.' They duly cut off the bristles and Miller had his way. A couple of years earlier the father of one of the Modernaires, Chuck Goldstein, died after a stroke.When Miller heard he took Goldstein out to the Variety Club, ordered up a couple of bottles and spent the night comforting the bereaved youngster. 'He was like a father to me that night', Goldstein has said.

Glenn Miller was infinitely more contradictory in his life than he ever was in the way he died. Paradoxi cally the impression is otherwise. His public image, backed up by those schoolmaster's wire-rimmed glasses, is one of the martinet, with occasional lapses for savage drunkenness. His death, in fact so simple, is shrouded in all the lurid imaginings a sensation-hungry press could muster.

Above all, Miller was a perfectionist. The problem was that try as he might, that perfection was never really achieved. In this simple clash of aim and achievement can be found the source of all the man's contradictions. Ever since his Mom had coached him in the slogans of mid-Western ambition, Glenn Miller had set his sights right at the top. But ever since he quit the Pollack Band to make way for a lifelong trombone-playing rival, and indeed superior, he had believed his ability was flawed. Jack Teagarden was always just the bit better. Even when Miller was invited to join *Metronome's* All-Star Band for 1941, he only made it to the trombone chair because Teagarden, the number one choice, was unavailable. Then there was his band. Everyone who played in it, and the more dispassionate of those who heard it, agree with a simple fact: the band was technically perfect, it moved like a perfectly oiled and tuned engine, but like so excellent a machine, it was perilously low on sponneity. Miller was continually praising the hot swinging style of a band like Basie's. He claimed never to understand why *his* musicians couldn't swing like the Count's. But even though the Miller outfit was never really designed as a killer-diller swing band, surely Miller must have seen the overall looseness, the free flow of ideas, the spontaneously generated arrangements that typified a band like Basie's and which never even started to touch his own musicians.

It wasn't that the individual musicians lacked talent. Sure enough, compared with the

Goodman alumni, Krupa and James, or Artie Shaw's Tony Pastor, there were few topflight spinoffs from the Miller sidemen. This, on the other hand, was as much due to Miller's ability to stay right in with the money and thus keep men with him, as it was to the lack of sparkle among individuals. Still, it's fair to say that Miller was never one to hire the great individualistic stars. Quite honestly, he didn't want them. What he wanted were competent musicians who were young enough to be influenced and not so established or egocentric as to break out of the controls he established. The two anecdotes cited above, and the host of others that make up an integral part of the Glenn Miller story show time and time again that Miller relished this paternal role. And he wasn't a liberal father, either. Maybe it was his own relatively shiftless, incompetent father who made him determine on a personal remedy for childhood loss, but Miller's paternalism was of the 'spare the rod and spoil the child' variety. If you stepped out of line, there would be trouble. Maybe Glenn couldn't bring out the strap, but dismissal would always substitute.

There was another side, of course, Miller could be very generous and kind to his musicians. Whenever they were in trouble, he would be there with a friendly word, a loan, a few days' respite from work. Deaths always seem to have brought the best out of him. They were his 'children', their sorrows were his. After all, until he and Helen adopted their two children, Miller had no children of his own. All the more reason to turn parental attitudes towards all those young musicians. The fans, too, benefited from Miller's generous side. While unscrupulous promoters would capitalise on the kids' adulation of the band to charge extra-high prices for Miller shows, Glenn ordered that his concerts were to cost a dollar plus tax and not a penny more. Unless, of course, the promoter has his permission in writing.

There was another, more practical side to Miller's handling of his musicians that transcends the disciplinary aspects. If he wanted them all to wear two-tone Florsheims, keep their hair short and have no more than the allotted inches of handkerchief showing above

ABOVE: Goodman and Gene Krupa clowned for the cameras, but backstage no-one was laughing. Autocratic Miller tried to keep the army band up to scratch by amputating their moustaches. It didn't make anyone particularly happy. Anyway, discipline wasn't 'the General's' real problem in the first place. Nemesis Jack Teagarden (*BELOW*) just wouldn't stop swinging out of the musical woodwork.

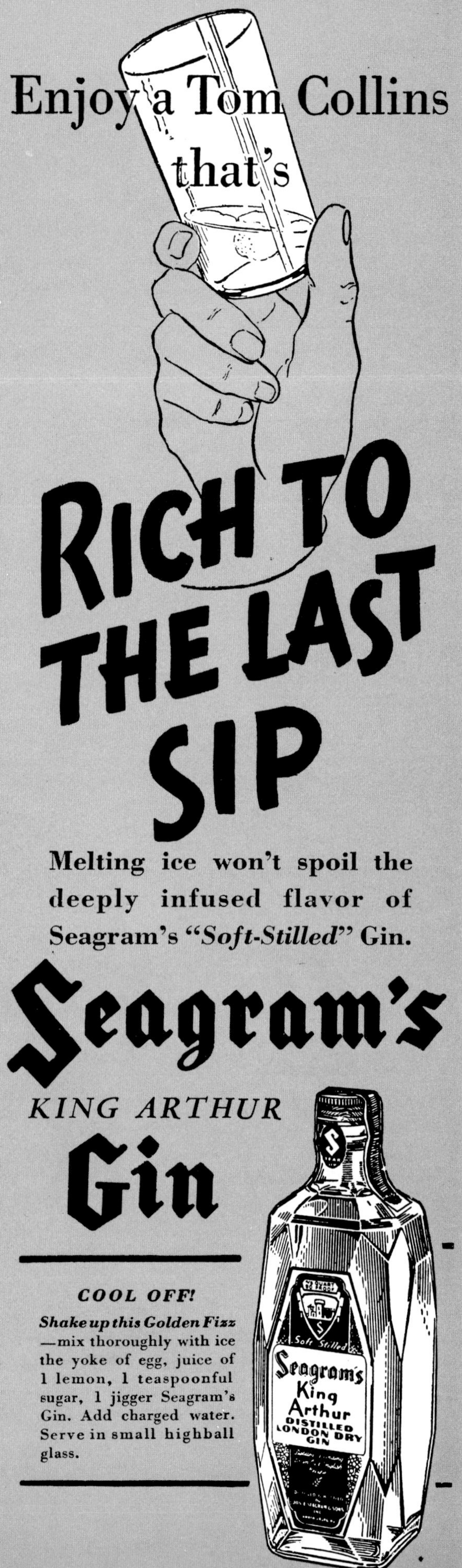

their breast pocket, well, that wasn't the end of the world. They were making good money for sidemen—$150 a week by 1941—and suffer ing a few onstage foibles wasn't all that bad. The real difficulties with Miller's treatment of musicians was that in the end he lacked a leader's essential talent. It was alright creating a well-drilled machine, but many of the musicians themselves, not to mention the legions of critics, felt that Miller was never really tapping the potential of his bandsmen. It stemmed, of course, from his insistence on having musicians who would do what they were told. A talented soloist would find himself submerged in the general massy weight of the 'Miller sound'. Miller's favourites held sway, irrespective of talents. Tex Beneke could never play sax with the verve and originality of his number two man, Al Klink, but Klink was never given any real chance to shine. Perhaps it was Miller's own fear of stars eclipsing his appeal yet again. Few of the real stylists who came to the Miller band stayed that long. Either they quit or Miller fired them. Toeing the line, coming up to the Miller standards, the same virtues as sustained the boss himself, were what counted. Blowing some exquisite solo was less vital.

The case of both Miller's singers, Marion Hutton and Ray Eberle, prove the extent to which Miller preferred to take the second rate and mould it, obtaining the best and giving it a chance to flourish. Bob Eberly, who was given his head by Jimmy Dorsey, made an uninspiring band into a winner simply because his talent was allowed its full range. Brother Ray, whose talents were not that great in the first place, but was hired because he was Bob's brother and right in the Miller mould, served only to demean some of Miller's performances. At the end, whether it was his excusses of Miller's intransigence that caused the final break, there was a third party to the argument. The band was fed up with his failings and wanted him out anyway. Marion Hutton, the very perfection of the girl next door figure that Miller wanted to offer his audience, was another who was marked for stardom by Miller but never really had the makings of a big star. If one looks at the crooners and canaries of the time and checks out the one who prospered in the post war decades, she is absent from the lists. Even at the time, Miller must have appreciated that with better stars he could have sold even more records. Too often a Miller version of some song would founder, while another leader, armed with stronger singers, would run away with the sales. It wasn't surprising that Tommy Dorsey's version of I'll Never Smile Again' should outsell Miller's; after all, he had Frank Sinatra up there at the mike. But Harry James 'Ciribiribin' wasn't intrinsically any better than Miller's. He just had stronger vocals.

Miller, of course, was pre-eminently an arranger. Even without the immense successes of his band in later years, the reputation he built up in the early and mid-Thirties would still put him amongst the important figures of the Swing Era. And undoubtedly many of the big Miller hits came from music and not words. 'Moonlight Serenade' is the obvious example, but all the great Miller recordings are the product of an arranging talent. Yet even with his arrangers, Bill Finegan, Jerry Gray and later Billy May, Miller was capricious and restrictive. He wanted no rivals, no independence even here. He had developed the Miller style and that was the way things were going to stay. No wonder Finegan, who later went on to join another top arranger, Eddie Sauter in the Finegan-Sauter band of the 1950s, and the others chafed under the Miller bit. By the time the band broke up in 1942 one of them, Billy May, had already started working on the side of Alvino Rey.

It was necessary, everyone admitted then, to have a degree of discipline in one's leading of a big band. There were a good number of musicians, the 300 plus mile a day hops needed tight scheduling and organisation, the long stays in New York put temptations, so leaders felt, in the way of their musicions. Whether this was justified to the extents Miller took it is another story. Fanatically loyal to his sponsor, Chesterfield Cigarettes, Miller always smoked them himself, and the bandboy was always on hand with a fresh pack whenever required. While the rest of the band might not share his taste, Miller checked every public appearance and whenever non-Chesterfield packs were visible, they would

When the big bands went under after the War, the top singers just kept working harder. Top of the tree was ex-Tommy Dorsey crooner Frank Sinatra (*ABOVE* in 'On The Town'). Sinatra went solo in 1942 after he believed rumours that his rival Bob Eberly was scheduled to go it alone. In fact the rumours fell through, but the young Sinatra never looked back. Eberly, once his main challenger, slipped insignificantly away.

Nat 'King' Cole was one of the few solo singers who hadn't graduated through the Swing bands. But he certainly knew a good thing when he heard it. Ex-Miller arranger Billy May (*ABOVE* with Cole) helped with several of the black star's hits.

ABOVE: **Big band stars never stayed put long. Goodman trumpeter Harry James (shown here in 'Springtime In The Rockies') quit to start his own outfit. James' band hit big: the boss married Betty Grable and discovered Frank Sinatra. He's still in there swinging.**

swiftly be covered by pieces of paper. He put together a massive list of instructions for his various managers—tour, road, business and personal—and made sure they kept to them. Basically a manual of rules and regulations, the managers were told to keep the band on time and together. There were plenty of fines for defaulters. But there was the positive side as well. No one-night stands should be more than three hundred miles apart—a conservative move in an era when hops of nearer four hundred miles were quite frequent—and that ticket prices should be kept down to a dollar plus tax. But the mass of rules didn't really promote the most easy-going of atmospheres. As such bands as Count Basie's had shown, one could be brilliant without such restrictions. When, at Christmas 1940, the band bought Miller a new Buick with the number 'GM—1' it appeared as if everyone loved him. But there was a public vote and the loyalists easily shamed the rebels. The Glenn Miller Orchestra was not a place for the loner.

Except, that is, for its leader. Miller, according to some of his intimates, was only a martinet for the sake of self-defence. Desperately keen to be needed, but simultaneously urging himself to higher and higher standards of perfection, Miller enclosed himself in a cast-iron protective armour. Occasionally he would come out. Sometimes it would be to lambast the band, taking their pros and cons publicly and one by one as he did with the AAF outfit in 1944. Or perhaps it would be in the golf course or during a game of touch football when his do-or-die competitiveness would cut through the give-and-take attitudes of his fellow players. Then again the Miller charm and generosity might get an airing, a favourite might be treated, an unhappy member given some reassuring chat.

One area of operations which showed Miller at his toughest was the world of business. If he could avoid the loose living that wrecked a leader like Bunny Berigan, then he wasn't about to fall into the slack business practices that ruined such stars as Gene Krupa whose personal talent was never matched by his fortunes fronting a band. Miller was not mean, nor was he greedy, but he was never willing to gain a little good will if it meant losing a little cash. The Palladium Ballroom fracas of 1941, when he vetoed the giving of free admission for the launch of 'Sun Valley Serenade' is a case in point, but it is one among many. Miller lived, as he always did, by the letter of the law. He was unable to appreciate that sometimes its spirit might prove a more useful rulebook. His futile attempts to gain a greater percentage of the agency's booking fees were just part of his determination to 'maximise the potential' of his and his band's appeal. It would be wrong, however, to discredit Miller's tough approach to business. It didn't take much intelligence to realise that if the band didn't play as tough as the sharks

ABOVE: Miller was the first to pay for rehearsal time. You couldn't ask for more. You certainly wouldn't get any.

around them, they only had themselves to blame. Miller was at the top of a tree from which the world, the entertainment world anyway, would have been happy to see him fall. As leading phenomenon of a phenomenal craze, the Glenn Miller Orchestra's top ranking was eternally up for grabs. It required only the toughest means and determination to keep it at the top. It was for this, no doubt, that the band, however disciplined, would always thank the leader they only half jokingly nicknamed 'The General'.

Glenn Miller cannot have been the easiest person to work for. His tough-guy mask made him frighteningly unapproachable, especially to youngsters to whom he could be deliberately aggressive, to make sure they appreciated the full onus of working in the Miller band. His habit of forming snap judgments was also less than help to making easy friendships. When Jimmy Abato was hired to play clarinet, Miller came out against him from the start. 'I don't like to hire Italians and Jews, they're troublemakers', stated the boss. Whether he meant this charmless crack or not, no-one really knows. Maybe at the time he did. But a checklist of the band shows that he would have had to fire half the personnel if he was going to stand by his dictum. It was full of both Jews and Italians and some of them, in the ever-popular phase, were his best friends. Or at least as good friends as he would permit.

And then there's one final question: just how good *was* the Glenn Miller Orchestra—Reading the critics at times, it might seem as if the phenomenal successes of the band were some kind of elaborate media trick. That Miller's band didn't really swing, that his singers were second rate and his soloists hampered by Miller's own rules, that everything that happened was just a mistake. For some of that, there is an element of truth. Compared, say, to the Basie band he admired so much, Miller's musicians weren't such a swinging outfit. But Miller never intended them to go all the way into the Swing idiom. His singers second rate? That has been dealt with above, though it was noticeable that when Miller relaxed the reins of Ray Eberle and slowed things down a little, it was surprising how much better he could sound. And of course Marion Hutton, with her cuter than cute appeal *did* bring the fans in, even if her singing was not up to Peggy Lee, Helen O'Connell and other great stars. And Miller did restrict his soloists. It is true. But on the other hand Miller had a sound, and a very commercial and successful sound, quite intentionally manufactured, which was not geared to elaborate, free-form solo efforts. Of course many might feel that restricting that degree of spontaneity is a mistake. One can only reply with the evidence of Miller's record-breaking popularity across the nation and, when the AAF band came to Europe, its spread around the world.

Miller was never given one of those nicknames—'The King of Swing', 'the Sentimental Gentleman of Swing'—but his fame was as great, if not greater than either Benny Goodman or Tommy Dorsey. His band reached a perfection of unified playing that may have become, in time, monotonous, but never failed to came up to standard. In the end, irrespective of the niceties of critical attention—and the more purist jazz critics dismiss Miller and *all* Swing bands as 'degenerate'—success can only be judged by public opinion. And the Glenn Miller Orchestra, from its Glen Island opening till its last show for Chesterfields, never lacked total, enthusiastic backing from America's swing fans. With his disciplined musicians and his legions of fans Glenn Miller may not have been Swing's monarch, but undeniably, he was its 'General'.

CHAPTER ELEVEN

MARCH TIME

BEDFORDSHIRE IS, to all intents and purposes, the middle of England. It's an unprepossessing county, relatively flat, with no special characteristics or dramatic geographical features. It has its small county town, smaller still over thirty years ago, its villages and farms and other smaller towns dotted around. After the bright lights of New York, it was an odd place for Glenn Miller and his new band to come. But war is no respecter of personal taste. Anyway for a midwestern boy like Glenn Miller, the midlands of England were as homely a place as any three thousand miles away from home.

Of course when Glenn Miller reported for his induction to the US Army Specialist Corps on October 7th, 1942, he was a very long way, emotionally, ideally and geographically from Bedford. He was full of plans for the future. All the great musicians who had been drafted would be redrafted, this time with him as the director of operations, into a number of first-class bands. They would be used to entertain the troops around the country and in due course somewhat nearer the front lines. His ideas worked (Millers' always did) but the Army, being the Army, had different ones.

Glenn Miller made a terrible recruit. In the first place there was the sickening dive from being the country's most popular bandleader to joining the ranks of all those other new soldiers getting their basic training. To add to his problems Miller was drained, physically and emotionally after what amounted to three years' virtually nonstop performing, recording, wheeling and dealing. It was fine so long as the band was working; pure instinctive nervous energy kept him going. The routine of army life had no such pick-you-ups. It was dull, it was boring, and in the end infantry training was unlikely to be of much use to a man whose most potent weapon would be his trombone.

Such reservations cut no ice with the military. They had their methods and that was that. Tempo had always been taught by 'watching the bouncing ball' films. It was absurd, it drove 0505273 Miller round the bend, but that was the Army way. So was the endless shuffling of Miller around the country part of the Army style. Inducted in New Jersey, he went rapidly, sometimes with no more than a few hours' stopover, from Maryland, to Omaha, to Alabama. It was at Maxwell Field, Alabama, that he was given his first assignment, Special Services Officer.

There was one more move in store for Miller before he could even start to put any of his new plans into operation. Strangely enough the Army had ignored the real status of its new volunteer recruit. It was not until basic training was over, and Miller was beginning to get moved around just like the bouncing ball he'd been watching on the G.I. screen, that a branch of the Army, the AAF (Army Air Force) realised just who they had on their hands. Without letting on to the rest of the organisation, the AAF quietly put in a request for Captain Miller's transfer from Alabama to the AAF HQ at Knollwood, North Carolina. No sooner said than done. Miller was appointed Director of Bands Training for Army Air Forces Technical Training Command (AAFTTC).

Which was where his troubles began. The first thing Miller wanted to do was start putting together the quality Army bands he'd been planning for months. But it seemed as if the Army had other ideas. Just because he had been so big deal a band leader in civilian life, Miller shouldn't expect to ride roughshod through Army traditions just like that. No way. All the barriers that jealousy, stupidity and the simple fear that bedevils veteran career officers still desperate for promotion were put in Miller's way. Every suggestion he made was blocked by some malignant spirit. For a start he just concentrated on getting together some of his old band.

Not all of them wanted to come. Tex Beneke was in the Navy and had no intention of quitting. Bill Finegan wanted to stay in the air force and Willie Schwartz too was happy as a sailor. Some, on the other hand were delighted to join their old leader again. The rigours of infantry life were hardly conducive to much pleasure. For a man who had recently been enjoying even the restricted freedoms of the big band world with Glenn Miller, the opportunity to rejoin him was a godsend. Trigger Alpert, Zeke Zarchy and Jimmy Priddy all made their way via memo and command and counter-command to Miller's AAFTTC unit. By continual scrutiny of the draft registers, and by making sure that soon-to-be-drafted musicians gave him good warning, Glenn Miller was able gradually to assemble a good nucleus of top Swing musicians around him. One by one the stars of the

ABOVE: Miller never really got on with the BBC hierarchy. Scheduled for a BBC series, he jettisoned it after a week when the red tape, yet again, proved too absurd. But England still enjoyed the Miller band on AFN. Still, he was happy to move on towards conquered Europe, when Eisenhower (*LEFT*) called him across the Channel to liberated France.

Many of the big leaders plied their most useful trade through the War. Miller (*BELOW*) was perhaps the best known, but others, like Artie Shaw and Claude Thornhill (*ABOVE*) did more than just their bit. In the States and abroad, on stage and on the free V-discs issued specially for the troops, the big bands kept playing. Maybe they were in uniform. So what. What did they think their audiences were wearing?

big bands were drawn into the Army, and one by one they gravitated to Glenn Miller, now based at New Haven and using the Yale University campus for rehearsals.

The AAFTTC band included some of the best swing musicians available. Benny Goodman's band had contributed Mel Powell (piano), Chuck Gentry (sax) and Steve Steck (trumpet). Bernie Privin (trmp) and Hank Freeman (sax) were drafted away from Artie Shaw. Claude Thornhill, one of the leaders with Miller backing, sent along his bass Marty Blitz, and a drummer, Gene Leman. From Tommy Dorsey's stand came guitarist Carmen Maestren. It was a diverse, but talented assembly. And there was the Miller team of Ray McKinley, Alpert, Priddy and Zarchy who was made First Sergeant. Arranger Jerry Gray also turned up in uniform.

It was Gray who sparked off Miller's celebrated run-in with an irate Major. McKinley and another arranger Perry Burgett had been fooling around, mixing a little of their own music with the sort of fodder the Army bands, reared only on Sousa marches, provided them. The idea of swing marches was born. Jerry Gray was called in by Miller and suddenly a whole new idiom was created. 'The St Louis Blues March' was the order of the day. It was not universally applauded. One apoplectic Major turned on Miller. 'Look, Captain Miller, we played those Sousa marches straight in the last war and we did alright, didn't we?' 'Yessir,' snapped Miller, 'you certainly did. But tell me one thing: are you still flying the same planes as you did in the last war, too?' The swinging marches remained.

Bucking the brass was not enough. Miller wanted positive steps, not negative ones. And so did his band. A group of rebels started to form. Mel Powell and Peanuts Hucko among them, they couldn't stand the Army's love of discipline. Given the extra fillip of Miller's love of rules and regulations, they found life in the AAFTTC Band increasingly restrictive. The episode when Miller decided to have everyone cut off their moustaches was supremely irritating. While for him it was just one way of working off his own frustrations on his band, a means of relief made even easier by the yawning gulf between the rights of officers and those of their men, for the men so deprived it was more than just an affront to their vanity. Playing reeds or brass with a moustache requires a different style to playing it without. On a purely professional level, and Miller always attempted to be first and foremost a professional, it was a stupid blunder. Claiming that musicians had to be more soldierly than the other GIs and that the moustaches made them look like gangsters cut little ice.

A more creative move was the start of a new Glenn Miller radio show. The idea came much earlier, but official objections, ruling and over-rulings held up the launch until July 10, 1943. Called 'I Sustain The Wings' the programme was centred on Miller's band and featured dramatic interludes quite simply designed to attract more volunteers to the forces. It started with CBS but then transferred to NBC after six weeks. It stayed there for the next eleven months. On a typical show Miller would be introduced and then launch into a summary of the fortunes of the war abroad. His last show, June 10, 1944, opened like this: 'It's been a big week for our side. Over on the beaches of Normandy our boys have fired the opening guns of the long awaited drive to liberate the world. And over here the folks who are backing up those boys are staging another big push of their own, the Fifth War Loan Drive' . . . It was all corny stuff, but the music went down very well and the band toured the country backing War Bond rallies and making appearances for the troops still awaiting their orders to the fronts. From Miller's personal point of view, the big success of the radio show was the end of his tedious work as Bands Director for the AAFTTC. That onerous task was given out to someone else and Miller became responsible only for his radio show. By April 1944 he had gained almost total autonomy over his personnel. Under the title 2001st Base Unit (Radio Production) the band became responsible to Miller and not to the HQ at Yale.

Once again, the success and growing independence of Miller did not go unnoticed among his more jealous colleagues. One attempt was made to stop the issue of any more V-discs, the free records made for issue to serving troops in camps at home and abroad, with Miller's name on them. It was felt that to make him too popular would be a mistake. It was not for nothing that Miller fumed about 'conspiracies' when he found out. Needless to say the flow of V-discs from the AAF band under Captain Miller was not stopped. But a vast number of his plans were quashed. All, that is, except for one. And that was the one that really mattered to him.

Miller really wanted to see the AAF band in Europe. Continually, but with no luck, he pestered his superior officers for a chance to take his men to England and from there perhaps to newly re-conquered France. Time

Glenn Miller was called 'The General' before the war ever touched America. He may have only been a Captain when he went into uniform in 1942, but his naturally autocratic style really fitted army life. With his sense of the social divide, the gap between officers and troops was ideal. Of course the 'troops', or rather his drafted musicians, weren't so keen on the idea. Army discipline was hardly welcomed by freewheeling bandsmen. Arranger Perry Burgett and ex - Goodman pianist - cum - arranger Mel Powell (*ABOVE*) were just a couple of the AAF Band who rebelled against Miller's methods. It didn't get them anywhere. Just a personalised dressing-down from Miller and a threat no-one wanted to buck. Reduction to the ranks — the ones that had to fight!

and again he was turned down, but when the 2001st Base Unit (Radio Production) was formed with Miller at its head, the way seemed clear. Almost at once he started putting together the personnel he intended to take with him to the UK. Musicians, technicians, radio actors, arrangers, road managers . . . altogether he selected some sixty-two people for the trip.

On June 10th, 1944, Miller and the AAF Band played the last of their 'I Sustain the Wings' shows. It had been a highly successful series. At one show in New York the band had encouraged pledges of $2,300,000. Two consecutive appearances in Chicago and St. Louis had netted $4,000,000 worth of pledges each. One could see why the authorities were trying to keep Miller on the job at home. But he had set his sights on Europe.

On June 13th the first 'buzz bombs', the V-1 rockets, landed on London. Only five days later a more welcome arrival came to the city: Glenn Miller. His band, after a couple of days of signing forms, extending their arms for shots and innoculations, and bidding farewell to various loved ones, embarked on what was known to the Army as NY8425, in more civilised terms, the Cunard liner, Queen Elizabeth. For the six-day crossing from New York to the Firth of Clyde in Scotland, the band played for the 17,000 troops who were making the journey with them. Sometimes there were relays of musicians, all taking the same instrument. As one saxophonist had to rush off and vomit over the side, another would step in smartly and keep the party going.

They arrived in London on July 1st and found themselves quartered at 25 Sloane Street, right in the path of the worst of the flying bombs and known to Londoners as 'Buzz Bomb Alley'. It only took one night of cowering in subterranean bomb shelters for Miller to make determined representations to the powers that be. It was all very well bringing the band to play for the troops, but it wasn't so good having them blown up before they could play a note. Authority, for once moving speedily, agreed. On July 2nd Miller and his band were shifted to the Co-Partners Hall in Bedford, owned in peacetime by the Gas Board and used for the duration as an emergency studio

And the band played on... 'The Glenn Miller Story', faithful as ever to the myths, had the AAF lineup swinging for rapturous Britons come rain, shine or bombers. In fact the last thing Miller wanted was casualties on the bandstand. On arrival in London the band

of the BBC.

On July 9th the band, renamed 'Captain Glenn Miller and His American Band of the Supreme Allied Command' started broadcasting to the troops they had come to entertain. They put out shows for the BBC and the Allied Expeditionary Forces Network. The former lasted but a week. With the depressing insularity of the British civil servant, Maurice Gorham, who was supposedly liaising with Miller, informed him that changes in the band's volume of playing had worried many BBC listeners on the fringes of transmission areas. When the band was loud it was fine, but when it went soft they feared that the BBC had gone off. And for the BBC to go off, especially in wartime and even though Jerry *was* on the run, was tantamount to the collapse of civilization. Therefore, Miller was asked, could the band play at a constant level of volume!? Miller

was billeted right in the heart of the buzzbombs. 'The General' soon had them moved to rural Bedfordshire, out of the bombers' range. When it came to his own skin, Miller may have worried about death, but never really concentrated enough on self-preservation.

was never known for taking the subtle approach to a problem when the blunt one would do. Rather than reasoning with the hapless BBC man, he merely told him that forthwith the Miller broadcasts would be restricted to the Forces Network and that the BBC could live without him. He then turned on his heel and stalked off.

For the Forces, however, Miller and his musicians provided a wide variety of shows. Apart from the broadcasts by the whole ensemble, there was 'Swing shift', dance music played by Ray McKinley and a seventeen piece band, 'Uptown Hall', a small jazz combo, 'A Soldier and a Song' and a self-explanatory 'Strings with Kings'. All of which were an immediate success with radio audiences around the country. But that was by no means the limit of Miller's activities. During the year the band played in Europe, both in France and England they made some 800 performing appearances, either live or on the radio. In the five and a half months while Miller still led them, there were some 71 live concerts. They were watched by an audience of around 247,500 extremely appreciative servicemen. Once again, the Miller success story was pulling in the telephone numbers.

There was one aspect of life in England that Glenn Miller hated. The band moved across country not in a bus but in their own airbus, a C-47. Miller hated flying. Sometimes, in conversations with his intimates he would speculate on the likelihood of his death in a plane. He was becoming increasingly home-sick as the months went by. He didn't like the food, and indeed wartime England was worlds away from the marginal economies that Americans back home claimed were their wartime hardships. He didn't want his meat, what little meat there was, cooked the way the English cooked it. He missed his glasses of iced water with everything. They were petty frustrations, but Glenn had never reacted very cheerfully for any setbacks. He had come to do a job, but now he felt there should be some developments. An avid disciplinarian himself, he chafed under restrictions that were not of his own making. In the end his problems were just like those of everyone else who had got caught up in the war. And like them, he was full of plans for what would be done when he got back home. The first post-war show would be at the Paramount where he had already started negotiating a guarantee of a massive $15,000 per week. He would work with the band six months of every year and devote the rest of the time to other lucrative activities. First of all he planned to buy into the Coca Cola company's millions by taking on a tri-state distributorship. Then he saw himself running a chain of motels. There would be prestige concerts in the world's top halls. The Glenn Miller Orchestra would be the biggest of all the big bands. And there was 'Tuxedo Junction', the ranch-house he had planned for building in California. He had a model of it made while he was in Bedford and the boys in the band would often find him gazing optimistically at it, looking forward more and more to the day when he could get back home.

In August 1944 he was summoned to Paris by the Supreme Allied Command HQ. Would he be prepared to take over the directorship of the US Army Band? He rejected the offer out of hand. Let the marching bands keep marching, he had better things to do. It was a brief interview and Miller promptly flew back to London. August was a phenomenally busy month for his band. They toured some 35 bases and recorded and played forty-four broadcasts over the radio. Apart from his homesickness, the constant pressure was affecting his health. As the summer wore on into Autumn, Miller's temper grew thinner by the day. The only good news as far as he was concerned was, that as of August 17th, Captain Miller had been promoted to Major Miller.

On November 15th a ray of sun flooded into his increasing gloom. Another summons to SHAEF in Paris. This time the interview ran along the lines Miller had wanted. He and the band were to come to Paris for six weeks to entertain the troops who had been fighting in France. Was he interested? He certainly was. He was ordered to France, 'by command of General Eisenhower' on or about December 14th. The next month was the busiest the band had had yet. Apart from their regular shows, they had to pre-record another six weeks worth so that their British fans would stay entertained on the air while they were over playing in France. They recorded eighty-five thirty minute shows in eighteen days. It was a phenomenal effort. It also frayed tempers more than ever. One day Miller assembled the whole unit and started systematically tearing strips off each and every one of them. He did it cruelly, unmercifully and, what was worst of all, publicly. Defaulters, and everyone seemed to fall somehow into that category, were threatened with a new career, in the infantry, if they didn't mend their ways. It was hardly calculated to endear the General to troops who were already doing their damnedest.

On December 14th there was thick fog shrouding the whole of Britain. Miller was in London at the US Officers Club where he met Colonel Norman Baesell. Baesell, keen to show he didn't give a damn for weather of any sort, told Miller he was scheduled for a Paris trip the next day. Why not come along. He was flying in General Goodrich's own personal plane, a C-64 Norseman and the pilot, Flight Officer Johnny Morgan was one of the best flyers the USAF possessed. How about it?

Miller hated flying in the best of weather. He also knew that thick fog and maybe ice were hardly conducive to a comfortable, warm or even safe flight in a tiny plane like the Norseman. But there was something else he knew and it mattered more than any practical considerations. A lifetime's training had drilled into him the qualities he equated with perfectionism, with being a leader, and a soldier for his country. One did not show fear. Not only that, there was a direct order from General Eisenhower, the Supreme Commander himself. When Baesell made his invitation to Miller, the Major had no option but to accept.

The next day dawned as foggy as the one before. The regular SHAEF shuttle was still grounded and in the thick fog, it didn't even look as if the birds were bothering to take off, let alone the aeroplanes. Baesell arrived full of optimism. There was no need to worry. Maybe it was a bit foggy up here in Bedfordshire, but once away down south . . . they'd be in Paris in no time.

Miller was apprehensive but he was also impatient. He strolled, very jittery around the tarmac. Baesell kept telling him it would all be fine. Suddenly they heard the whine of a motor. It sounded as if the plane it came from was searching aimlessly for the airstrip. But there it was, gliding down out of the fog. Like it or not, it looked as if Miller would be flying that day after all. Baesell led the way into the plane. Miller said a few goodbyes and told Zeke Zarchy he'd see him in Paris. As he stepped into the plane eye-witnesses heard his exclaim, 'Hey! where the hell are the parachutes?' Baesell replied, his voice full of devil-may-care bravado, 'What's the matter Miller, do you want to live for ever.' The single engined nine-seater plane lumbered off into the fog, rose and vanished.

Three days later, when the rest of the band flew over to Paris, the weather couldn't have been more perfect. The flight was quick and easy and the only problem came when they touched down at Orly airport. Where was

On stage, in recording studios and for radio shows, Miller slaved away his months in Britain.

Glenn, who had promised to see them on arrival? No-one accepted what was obviously the truth, that Glenn Miller had vanished over the Channel in rotten weather and flying in a plane unfit for that weather. They waited, hoping against hope, but Miller never reappeared. On December 23rd Helen Miller was told that her husband was missing. For the musicians, with or without Glenn, life, and the performances that were expected of them, had to go on. It took a few days before everyone accepted that Glenn would not be coming back. It was not a happy thought. Ray McKinley took over the band and took it through the rest of their tour of duty in Europe. When the band came back to New York on August 12, 1945, the banner that announced them over the side of the ship read 'Glen Miller'. The 'n' of his name was only a symbolic reminder of their absent leader.

It would be great fun to look over the rumours of Glenn Miller's possible whereabouts today and find some credibility in one of them. From the people who claimed Miller is alive, hideously scarred, in some Mid-West sanatorium, to those who claim to have found the remains of his C-64 deep beneath the Channel; from those who claim that Baesell was involved in black-marketeering and killed Miller, the pilot, and then mistakenly, himself; to those who have placed Miller in the hands of some Communist plot; there are hordes of wonderfully fanciful rumours to deal with his death of December 15th, 1944. The truth is depressingly simple. In the first place the weather was far too bad on a purely visual level for a small plane to plunge about in such dense fog. In the second the Norseman did not have any de-iceing equipment. This meant that if it flew above the weather it would freeze up, if it flew in it there would be zero visibility, and thus it was forced below it, perilously close to the treacherous surface of the Channel. In the third place the flight took place on the eve of the Battle of the Bulge; there was strict radio silence enforced, even though there was no sign of enemy planes anywhere in that area. And fourthly there is the human element. Baesell was too keen to get across the Channel for his own safety, not to mention his passengers'. Flight Officer Morgan, who had all that experience, should have used it to call

BELOW: From air to eternity! The single-engined C-64 Norseman that ferried Miller to his date with destiny – December 15th, 1944.

LEFT: The Miller Band were in Europe just over a year, but they packed in an unimaginable number of shows. With over 800 gigs of every sort, it meant the band were playing on average two shows a day! 300 concerts and 500 radio shows kept everyone busy. There were always willing helpers. Vanderbilt graduate Dinah Shore, Eddie Cantor's own discovery, doubled with Miller on a London bandstand. *FACING PAGE:* The real Frances Longford and the Modernaires recreate 'Chattanooga Choo-Choo' for the 'Glenn Miller Story'.

the flight off, Baesell's cajoling notwithstanding. And Glenn Miller, who hated flying, anyway, should have had the sense to forget his pride and admit that he wasn't risking his life in a pea-souper. Unfortunately for his band, his fans, his family and of course himself, Glenn Miller decided to take off that fateful day.

The myths still roll, like that December fog, about Glenn Miller's absent head. How did he die, how good was the band, what would have happened if he had lived? Perhaps what really matters was what he did when he was alive. The speculation is in the final asessment a luxurious waste of time.

Today's renewal of public interest in Glenn Miller is as good a testimony of his capabilities and his band's appeal as any sceptic might demand. It is over thirty-two years since Miller vanished, and the sound that he helped create is still as potent as ever. Listen to 'Moonlight Serenade' today . . . the emotion comes flooding back with every phrase of that eloquent theme tune. Whether he would have survived the drastic decline of Swing in quite the opulent style his homesick fantasies created is of course debatable. Yet the careers of Benny Goodman, Woody Herman and Artie Shaw, not to mention the masses of 'sweet' bands who survived the post war years, have survived very well despite Elvis, the Beatles and other demands on the successive generations of young music-loving fans. Swing was as much the music of the late-Thirties and of the War years, as rock and roll dominated the Fifties and the Beatles held sway a decade later. And Glenn Miller, with his hundreds of thousands of record sales, his nation wide radio broadcasts, his non-stop series of sell out concerts, and even his hackneyed movies (just like those which today's bands sometimes make) was the epitome of Swing.

In Miller's heyday, Swing had the field almost completely to itself. That today, when the diversity of musical forms is so much more varied, Miller's music is still pulling in new fans and delighting the older ones, shows just how good he was. But then that isn't surprising. For, as everyone knows, in the end, class always tells. Glenn Miller, for all his foibles and frustrations, his puritanism and pettiness, always, invariably, had class.

Ina Ray Hutton and Her Melodears. Her all-girl lineup was best forgotten, but later on curvy Ina Ray pulled in some men and the band kept improving.

CHAPTER TWELVE

END OF AN ERA

GLENN MILLER DIED when the going was good. Nobody could have convinced his grieving family and the legions of fans, but it was true. In December 1944 the Swing Era was still riding high. Perhaps the draft depleted the bands, but the forces had benefited where the civilian public had lost out. Apart from Miller's AAF Band, Claude Thornhill and Artie Shaw led their bands around the bases and the barracks at home and abroad. The Swing gospel had spread wherever American forces had gone, and by 1944 that meant most of the world. Back home the musicians who had escaped the draft kept the boom going. Fees rocketed, and audiences still flocked in; the optimism of the New Deal era had been boosted by Swing, now the diehard spirit of those fighting World War II found both sentiment and satisfaction from the same music.

Yet little more than two years after Glenn Miller had flown off into the Channel fog, the great Swing craze was tottering on its last legs. In January 1947 eight top bands were broken up. Benny Goodman, Woody Herman, Harry James, Tommy Dorsey, Les Brown, Jack Teagarden, Benny Carter and Ina Ray Hutton—every one a household name—disbanded within a brief month. It was a crippling blow to a musical movement that had boasted hundreds of bands at its height and which, so short a time before had seemed so indefatigably secure.

So what exactly went wrong? Who or what dragged the rug out from under all those Swing stars? Two sets of reasons: internal and external, the problems Swing had developed within its own organisation and the pressures that were moving against it from elsewhere.

The first internal tremor to hit the Swing bands was naturally the war. That wonderful year of 1942, when WNEW's Top Twenty sounded like a rollcall of the great was simultaneously the turning point for Swing. War had been declared on Japan and Germany the previous December and soon the draft began to bite into the bands. The first leader to go was Dean Hudson, certainly not a name figure, but as the months went by the net dragged in such stars as Artie Shaw, Alvino Rey, Ray McKinley, Claude Thornhill, Bob Crosby and of course Glenn Miller who distinguished himself by volunteering for the Army. Initially it may not have seemed that important. There were certainly plenty of ineligible leaders, such as Benny Goodman whose sciatica rendered him 4-F, and the flood of keen sidemen was only partially tapped by the draft. Still, as the war progressed, the drain on big band resources began to make itself felt. The service bands, collected by such leaders as Miller, Shaw and Thornhill, made sure that those sidemen and soloists who were drafted kept playing together, but back home the musicians and leaders began gradually to feel the wartime pinch.

In the first place the needs of frontline troops meant that as far as the civilian population were concerned several vital supplies were severely rationed. Petrol, an essential for any band's day to day transportation, was cut back. Inevitably the masses of tours, with their nightly hops of 300 miles and more, were cut back. On top of this the US Government slapped a solid 20% entertainment tax on everyone who owned ballrooms, theatres and the like. Once again, this meant problems for the bands. Big venues rode out the costs, and the public, always spending heavily in a crisis, absorbed some of the tax. It still meant that the smaller operators, always working on a thin margin of profit, were forced out of business. In turn the smaller bands were forced to the wall through a lack of bookings.

The converse of these cutbacks was that for many musicians, and leaders too, they were a benefit. If tours were wasteful of petrol, fine. Why not combine a little patriotism—especially necessary from those who had avoided the draft—with leisure and cut them out altogether. And if ballrooms were getting scarce, then that's fine too. The best thing for a musician and his band to do was choose a solid, safe, and above all well-paid venue and settle there. If the public wanted to hear the music, then they could damn well turn up where it was available. As the draft took more and more sidemen, those who were left realised the potential of the situation and exploited it without mercy. Petrol shortages didn't help the availability of venues either, since the public couldn't use their precious supplies driving out to the Glen Island Casino or Meadowbrook. These two leading ballrooms of the era, once packed every night that a band was featured, were forced to shut. They just weren't convenient enough. To top off the

LEFT: The draft decimated the big bands, but surviving the ravages of war was easier than withstanding those of time. Guns, bombs and the cacophony of battle were the least of their problems. Xavier Cugat and Harry James, flanked by canary Gloria De Haven and actress June Allyson (who later portrayed Helen Miller) survived the holocaust, but the majority, like Bob Crosby (_ABOVE_), weren't so lucky. By 1942, when the bands were peaking, the rot had set in. The big publishers, ASCAP and BMI, were fighting. The war effort took over the valuable supplies of petrol, cutting out the tours; and the materials that the bands used to press their records went to build the warplanes. Top ballrooms were forced to shut as customers conserved their precious gas supplies for priority travel. The cream of the musicians were dispersed through the forces. And to cap it all, American Federation of Musicians leader James C. Petrillo (_FACING PAGE_) fought the major record companies. For two years, as Decca, Columbia, RCA Victor and the rest stood adamant, the musicians boycotted their studios. The singers, independent of musicians, grabbed an eager audience. They never relinquished it. When the bands came home, they got all dressed up again, but no-one was offering them a place to go.

problems, the government set up a midnight curfew, known to all as 'the brownout'. It didn't exactly encourage people out late.

Soon a definite spiral had been created. The musicians set themselves up as valuable commodities and demanded wages to match. Leaders like Goodman could pull a personal $4,000 a night and top bands expected at least $7,500 for a week's shows. There seemed to be no end to it all. It was vital for the health of the popular music business, which was what Swing had become, that the spiral be broken. It was not apparently going to happen.

1942 also saw the start of another major attack on the security of Swing. For some time, and with due cause, the American Federation of Musicians, led by James C. Petrillo had been lobbying the big record companies for a higher rate of pay for their members when they worked in the studios. Repeated demands had come to nothing and even though Petrillo had promised 'no strikes,' the situation was so absurd in that year, when thousands of juke boxes and radio stations were using records without adequate royalty payments—musicians as a whole were facing dangerously high levels of unemployment. Petrillo called a strike on August 1 1942 and all recording was banned. The companies had no desire to accede to AFoM wishes at first and reacted to the strike merely by holding round the clock sessions through the last week of July. But by 1943 their backlog was eroded and first Decca, then Columbia and RCA Victor (in 1944) gave in and signed a contract with the Union.

Ironically the strike ended by doing more harm than good to the musicians. Recording, which was hoped to reach a peak of nearly 100,000,000 pressings in 1942 had already suffered when the government took over the bulk of the shellac supplies which were considered more vital for the war effort than for the recording studios. Now the strike cut back on releases even further. Inevitably the public looked elsewhere for their recorded entertainment. The first place that they turned was to those integral figures to the bands—their solo singers. The bands often needed the vocalists, but the reverse didn't hold true. By the time recording was reinstated in late 1944, the bands found that their old vocalists had now made a huge impact as solo artists and that they, the musicians, had lost plenty of ground.

The main recorded output in the war was in fact from the *V-discs*. Twelve-inch 78s with four or five numbers on each, they were the precursors of the modern LP. While the AFoM strike gutted the recording industry, the V-discs were naturally exempt. Between 1943 and 1948 the USA issued some 900 of them free to the troops. Often prefaced with a few words of encouragement from the bandleaders or singer in question, they spanned the full musical stage from Dixieland to Sweet and Swing to Hot Jazz. That their labels sometimes weren't wholly accurate never seemed to affect their morale-boosting properties.

ABOVE: **Woody Herman looked like a matinee idol, but his music proved him a real swinger. Robbed of the studios**

The business struggles within the music industry didn't centre on the AFoM strike. In 1941 the conservative and rather autocratic ASCAP (American Society of Composers, Authors and Publishers) had decided that the new medium, radio, should pay dearly for their use of ASCAP scores and lyrics. They owned, it is true, virtually all the copyrights on American music since 1884 but when in 1941 they decided to charge an annual $9,000,000 (double their old figure) for letting radio stations use their material. The networks refused to pay. Instead they responded by banning all ASCAP material and playing only what was owned by their own copyright company, BMI

by the strike, too much of Herman's early music has been lost. But the troops benefited: they always had V-discs.

(Broadcast Music, Incorporated, which had been set up to rival ASCAP in 1939). From January until October 1941 no ASCAP tunes were broadcast and in the meantime BMI built up some 36,000 copyrights from 52 publishers.

Both the BMI-ASCAP war, and the AFoM strike had primary, obvious setbacks for the big bands. In the first place they couldn't get airplay, many of them had registered copyrights through ASCAP. And in the second they couldn't get their material recorded. Neither of these situations could help their music or its continued popularity. But it is in the less obvious, secondary effects that these internecine squabbles really struck at Swing. If the main-stream big bands suffered during the two controversies, then the minority musical groups—country, known as 'hillbilly,' and blues, known as 'race'— benefited. Of the new BMI copyrights, very many were country or blues and while the major record companies fought Petrillo's Union, many smaller ones were started, quite happy to make terms with the AFoM and featuring not big band music, but hillbilly or race music. Add to this a final paradox and the reasons for Swing's rout grow clearer.

The third prong of the 'new' music's attack on Swing, the prevailing popular form of the time, came with that same New Deal which had helped the Swing craze reach such mammoth proportions in the first place. In an era when millions were starving, homeless and out of work and when to the more perceptive the world was falling into the hands of dictators and opressors, the sound of Swing was far from optimistic, it was trivial and insulting to the suffering masses. For the growing number of people who felt this way, the natural inclination was towards 'roots' music: protest and folk song, as well as the old-fashioned black slave blues. The WPA (Works Progress Administration), one of the New Deal's 'Alphabet Agencies', took an especial interest in researching and recording for posterity these old folk songs and the protest songs that every generation of struggling labour had thrown up from its ranks. Country, blues and now folk and protest—none of this looked for the Swing supremacy.

When the war ended, all the problems that had begun undermining Swing started to come together and make themselves felt. The vicious spiral of wage demands and the accelerating shutdown of easily accessible venues remained unbroken. Only now it started to backfire. The War years with their philosophy of eat, drink and be merry . . . were over. The public no longer had the stomach for such last-ditch leisure. Nor was there the money. Inevitably the bands suffered. Then there was the emergence of the vocalists as

A dozen bands gave up the struggle in January 1946. Ina Ray Hutton was just one more leader on the dole.

stars in their own right. No longer needing bands, they had struck out successfully on their own while the musicians were fighting the studios. Inevitably the bands suffered. And there was the emergence of TV as a new and immediately accessible forum of entertainment. Apart from the fact of getting several channels of entertainment at the turn of a dial, the big Swing outfits were considered too cumbersome for the little screen. Singers alone were fine. Inevitably, as ever, the bands suffered.

But with all these problems—the wages spiral, strikes, radio bans, solo artists emerging and the growth of TV—the Swing era would not have needed to plummet so fast after the war had it not been for the deeper problems that they had caused. It was the diversification of musical styles which these squabbles and selfishness had caused that really finished Swing so quickly. The bands had held sway for a respectable 25 years. In all fairness, they should have accepted that they couldn't go on for ever. Public taste just won't stand for it. But while they were on top, no-one wanted to consider a decline, even as it was already under way.

There was another side to the dismal picture as well. On a purely musical level, irrespective of strikes, squabbles, emerging country or blues forms, Swing as a style was collapsing from within. The big bands had established a style, and within it various sub-styles through their late-Thirties and early Forties heyday. Their problem was to move on without losing the public appeal of what the public had seen as swing. And in trying for this they found themselves caught between two opposing forces. On the one side were the ballroom operators. Petrol shortages, the entertainment tax and spiralling wages had given them enough problems. Now they were faced with musicians who, bored with years of producing the same, albeit successful music, didn't even want to play when they did have a venue and a crowd to fill it. Angrily they accused the musicians of playing over their audiences' heads, of ignoring anything but their own selfish whims. The musicians countered with cries of 'philistines', and there's no doubt that many operators were more interested in staying in the money than advancing the bounds of musical taste. But the boredom was there, and however justifiable it may have been, it helped the public just that little bit more.

The other force came from amongst the more rebellious of the musicians themselves. The new generation of young, creative talents, all of whom had grown up with the big bands, soon showed that they were turning away from their teachers. Just as the 'hot' playing of the late Twenties had challenged Sweet with Swing, so did the 'bop' rebels stand in their Harlem head-quarters at Minton's and toss *their* new discoveries into the face of Swing. As far as they were concerned Swing was played out. The new blood, the fresh enthusiasm which they might have injected into the form were diverted elsewhere. And the old brigade was fading fast.

By the start of the 1950s the big bands were already passing into history. Such greats as Harry James, Benny Goodman, Count Basie and of course Duke Ellington would forge on with new combos, assimilating what was new and useful and rejecting what they didn't need. And naturally there was always Guy Lombardo and the eternally corny Lawrence Welk. But the great days of the big bands, the glorious peak of the Swing Era was long gone. That disastrous month of January 1947 stripped out the heart when eight top units disbanded. From thereon in, the whole edifice simply crumbled to dust. Jazz, in its bop form, grew further away from straight popular music, and bop was duly supplanted by the avant garde performers who still rule today. The youth culture that had revolved around Swing, however faintly it might have been in the Thirties, grew in strength and potency to fill the halls for the rock 'n' roll revelations of the Fifties and the rock music that has developed ever since. Swing was essentially the music of its time and place. It should not be mourned. In any case, the best of Swing has stayed alive till today, in the works of Glenn Miller, Benny Goodman, Duke Ellington and the other greats. And to repeat once again the immortal phrase of the Duke himself, as applicable to today's Top Thirty as it was to the charts of forty years ago: 'It don't mean a thing, if it ain't got that Swing!'

INDEX

Page numbers listed in medium figures denote an important verbal reference. Page numbers entered in *italic* figures indicate both photographic and verbal reference.

DISCOGRAPHY

My first Glenn Miller record was a 78 r.p.m. 'miniature hurricane' Brunswick recording of "Tuxedo Junction" and "Moonlight Serenade".

Since that was released Miller had posthumously signed with R. C. A. Victor whose stately 33⅓ orange labled records now form the major part of my collection. A spokesman for the firm, Mr. Jonathan Morrish, has kindly supplied me with the current release data.

Glenn Miller—A Memorial (1944-1969) (6M1) *(8-track DPM8-1006. Cassette DPMK-1006)*

Glenn Miller—A Legendary Performer (DPM 2065) **Double album.** *(No 8-track or cassette)*

Glenn Miller and the Army Air Force Band (DHY-0004) *(Cassette DHYK-0004)* **(No 8-track)**

"The Nearness of You" and Others *(8-Track MP8-134. Cassette MPK-134)* **(No album)**

The Best of Glenn Miller, Vol. 3 *(8-Track MP8-100. Cassette MPK-100)* **(No album)**

Glenn Miller plays selections from *The Glenn Miller Story* and other hits *(8-Track MP8-120. Cassette MPK-120)* **(No album)**

The Legendary Glenn Miller Vol. 1 (LFM 1-7500) *(8-Track LFS1-7500. Cassette LFK1-7500)*

The Legendary Glenn Miller Vol. 2 (LFM2-7501) *(8-Track LFS2-7501. Cassette LFK2-7501)*

The Legendary Glenn Miller Vol. 3 (LFM3-7502) *(8-Track LFS3-7502. Cassette LFK3-7502)*

The Legendary Glenn Miller Vol. 4 (LFM4-7503) (8-Track LFS4-7503. Cassette LFK4-7503)

The Legendary Glenn Miller Vol. 5 (LFMS-7512) *(8-Track LFS5-7512. Cassette LFK5-7512)*

The Legendary Glenn Miller Vol. 6 (LFM6-7513) *(8-Track LFS6-7513. Cassette LFK6-7513)*

The Legendary Glenn Miller Vol. 7 (LFM7-7514) *(8-Track LFS7-7514. Cassette LFK7-7514)*

The Legendary Glenn Miller Vol. 8 (LFM-7515) *(8-Track LFS8-7515. Cassette LFK-7515)*

The Legendary Glenn Miller. Vol. 9. (LFM9-7516) *(8-Track LFS9-7516. Cassette LFK9-7516)*

The Legendary Glenn Miller Vol. 10 (LSA-3237) *(Cassette MPK-246)* **(No 8-Track)**

The Legendary Glenn Miller Vol. 11 (LSA-3238) *(Cassette MPK-247)* **(No. 8-Track)**

The Legendary Glenn Miller Vol. 12 (LSA-3239) *(Cassette MPK-248)* **(No. 8-Track)**

The Legendary Glenn Miller Vol. 13 (LSA-3240) *(Cassette MPK-249)* **(No. 8-Track)**

FACE THE MUSIC AND DANCE

O.K. FLATFOOT—You may dance a brilliant 'Bump', a horrendous 'Hustle'. You may look mean in your blue jeans and jacket—tough in your T-shirt!—but discard them! Discard them, I say. Dig out your old man's Zoot Suit, send your best girl to the barbers for a bee-hive and prepare to trip the light fantastic with this simple, "Fool-'em-it's-a-Foxtrot", type set. Not quite the real thing, but sufficient, with practice, to make Fred Astaire look like the Hunchback of Notre Dame. So put your arm round her waist, put on that style and grace, and away we go:

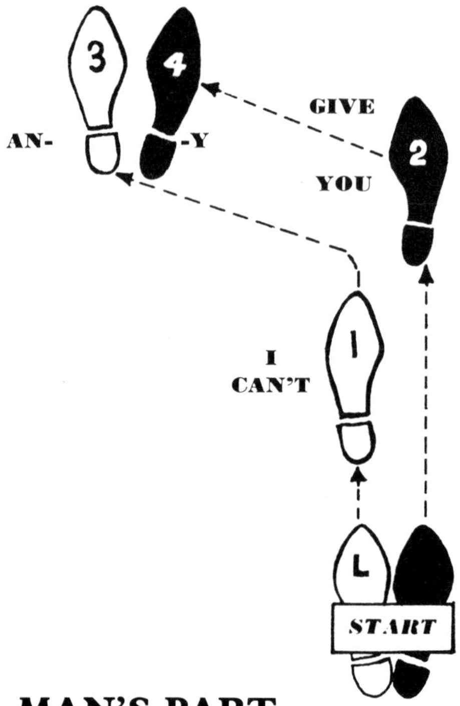

MAN'S PART

The man begins with his left foot.

1. *Left foot forward (slow).*
2. *Right foot forward (slow)*
3. *Left foot to the side (quick).*
4. *Right foot closes to the left (quick).*

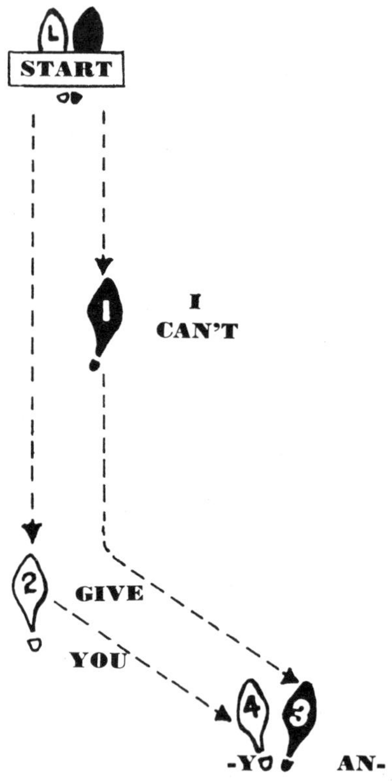

GIRL'S PART

The girl begins with her right foot.

1. *Right foot back (slow).*
2. *Left foot back (slow).*
3. *Right foot to the side (quick).*
4. *Left foot closes to the right foot (quick).*

O.K.! Practise that. When you're sufficiently pleased with your progress and tired of repeating endlessly "I can't give you anything but love . . ." try this Conversation Promenade, just to be flash!

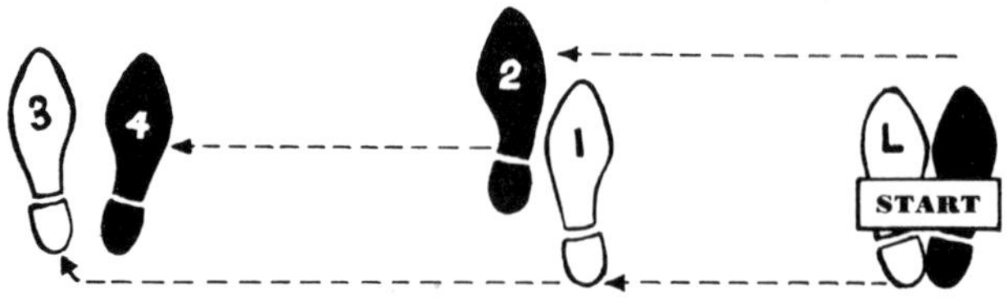

See you at the Palais

George Snow.